DID JESUS KNOW
HE WAS GOD?

FRANÇOIS DREYFUS, O.P.

Professor at the École Biblique
of Jerusalem

Translated from the French
by

Msgr. Michael J. Wrenn

THE MERCIER PRESS

THE MERCIER PRESS, 4 Bridge Street, Cork
24 Lower Abbey Street, Dublin 1

Did Jesus Know He Was God? by François Dreyfus, O.P.
Copyright © 1984 by Les Edicions du Cerf, 29 bd Latour-Maubourg, Paris. Translated from the French by Michael J. Wrenn. Copyright © 1989 by Franciscan Herald Press, 1434 West 51st Street, Chicago, Illinois 60609. All rights reservd.

This edition published by The Mercier Press, 1991.

ISBN 0 85342 943 X

Cover design: William Dichtl and Blane O'Neill, O.F.M.

Printed in Ireland by Colour Books Ltd.

Contents

Translator's Preface

The Dominican Francis Dreyfus was born in 1918. A graduate of l'*École Polytechnique* (France's equivalent of the Massachusetts Institute of Technology), Dreyfus was converted from Judaism to Catholicism and subsequently entered the Order of Preachers.

Since 1968, he has been professor of biblical theology at the renowned École Biblique in Jerusalem. For anyone familiar with the life of Père M.J. Lagrange, O.P., the founder of this world class seat of Catholic scriptural scholarship, it is fair to say that Father Dreyfus' approach to this vital question, *Did Jesus Know He Was God?*, profited greatly from the spirit, style, tone, and depth of scholarship of Père Lagrange.

It has been a privilege and an honor to have translated this work and to have become acquainted with this humble, self-effacing, and deeply spiritual lover of Jesus, our Lady, the Church, and the Scripture. May the reader of this work readily discover these qualities and apply them to his/her own efforts to assist Faith in Jesus to become living, conscious, and active through the light of instruction.

In conclusion, may I add that it was this type of rational but not *rationalistic* scholarship applied to the Scriptures that seemed to be called for during the January 1988 address in New York City on the *Crisis in Scriptural Interpretation* by Joseph Cardinal Ratzinger and in the various discussions that took place for two days as responses to the Cardinal's address. May this work also redound to the good of catechetical and homiletic efforts here and elsewhere.

Monsignor Michael J. Wrenn, M.A., M.S.
Pastor
St. John the Evangelist Church
Fifty-fifth St. at First Ave.
New York City
and Special Consultant for Religious Education
to John Cardinal O'Connor

Preface

Did Jesus know that he was God? "From a biblical view-point, this question is so badly phrased that it cannot be answered and should not be posed." In this fashion one of the most renowned Catholic exegetes expresses himself.[1] I am not of this opinion, and I would like to formulate this question in terms that are indisputably biblical. Let us suppose that, by some miracle, Jesus of Nazareth had in his hands, before his death, our Gospel according to St. John. How would he have reacted when faced with the words which the evangelist attributes to him: "No one has seen the Father, except the one who comes from God. He alone has seen the Father"; "Before Abraham was, I am"; "I and the Father are one"; "Father, glorify me with the glory that I had with you before the world existed" (6:46; 8:58; 10:30; 17:5)? Would Jesus have recognized in these affirmations some words, which even if he had not uttered them, he at least *could* have uttered because they corresponded to what he thought about himself, his person, and his mystery? Or would he instead have cried blasphemy and condoned those who, according to the evangelist, wanted to stone him precisely because of one of these declarations? Their reproach is clear: "Because being only a man, you make yourself God" (10:33).

For nearly seventeen centuries, from the time of St. John until the middle of the last century, Christians of every denomination would have shrugged their shoulders and, without any hesitation, would have responded "Yes" to the first question and "No" to the second, whether they were Catholic, Protestant, or Orthodox.

But when we read contemporary exegetical literature on the "Jesus of History," just as much from the Protestant side (for more than a century) as from the Catholic side (during recent decades), it indeed seems that the response would be exactly the opposite: "No" to the first question, "Yes" to the second. It is true that the question has never been formulated, so to speak, with such bluntness. But readers of this literature are led, almost by necessity, to pose it in terms very much akin to those I have employed. And the response that I have formulated, in their stead, seems to flow, by necessity, from the portrait of Jesus which is presenced by them.

Finally, other exegetes, reject my question by characterizing it as a false problem. They respond: We are able to attain the knowledge that Jesus had of his Person and his Mystery in merely one way: the historical-critical-exegetical study of the sources of the Gospels, which alone can yield, not the inner psychology of Jesus of Nazareth, but only words and behavior which, with some reasonable likelihood, can be attributed to him; even if, in their transmission, they have already become the object of a certain amount of interpretation. But nothing in these texts reveals anyone other than a prophet, a legate of God, even if he claims to have an intimate relationship with God, which is altogether unique. If Jesus had knowledge of his person more profoundly analogous to that which John attributes to him, he didn't say anything about it, and we, in turn, can say nothing about it. Moreover, they add, does the question have meaning? What significance does "knowing he is God" have for the man Jesus? Can we give this question understandable meaning which goes beyond words?

Unfortunately, regardless of whether this is a true or a false question, it is nevertheless a question that many Christians, after having read a particular work, listened to conferences or sermons on the person of Jesus of Nazareth, are raising. How many times have we heard comments of this type: "One frequently hears tell of Jesus, a free man, standing up against the established disorder, friend of those outside the law, etc. We are convinced that this is the way it is. But why do we never hear tell of the Jesus of St. John, unless it is to keep him on the level of the qualities described above"? If some people pose this question to a lecturer or to a preacher, they receive a response that goes somewhat like this: "I have spoken of the real Jesus, or one who appeared in the life and history of men, his contemporaries. The Jesus that you evoke is also a reality, but it is a theological reality which belongs to faith, not to history." Such answers often seriously disturb the faith of Catholics who correctly understand that this "theological reality" vanishes into myth if it does not have its source in the life, history, and knowledge of Jesus. Often, the reaction is fortunately that of a steady and robust faith: "We declare it each Sunday at Mass: Jesus Christ is true God and true Man. Just as the fact of being truly man implies that one have knowledge of it, so to be truly God, in the same way, implies for Jesus that he knows it." These Christians fully subscribe to the following statement of a contemporary exegete: "The personal knowledge of Jesus, the manner in which he conceived his person and his mission is what is most important to us in coming to the conviction that his disciples did not misrepresent his intentions and transform his real image."[2]

I am well aware that by responding "Yes," with great assurance, to the question which constitutes the title of this book that I will be treated as "a fearful fundamentalist," to use an expression of the Anglican Bishop J. A. T. Robinson, currently employed quite readily by some Catholic exegetes.[3] I am not a fundamentalist. For more than twenty-five years, I have been teaching Sacred Scripture, using all the scientific techniques which the advance of modern investigations has placed at the disposal of the exegete. I am not fearful; for the Catholic Church, at the service of which I am exercising my ministry as a professor of Sacred Scripture, has in several instances encouraged exegetes to stride forward with confidence on the basis of a twofold fidelity: on the one hand, a fidelity to the demands of a serious historical-critical-exegetical method; and on the other hand, fidelity to tradition and to the living magisterium of the Church.

My model will be that of Fr. Lagrange, founder of this École Biblique of Jerusalem in which I have had the honor of teaching for almost fifteen years. He has painfully lived out this twofold fidelity, and his positions on the question which is the subject of this book have lost nothing of their current value. In a number of instances, I will have occasion to refer to them.

In this short book, I want, as much as possible, to avoid engaging in polemics with one or another particular author whose ideas are, in my view, erroneous and with whom I will be taking issue.

Naturally, I will have to mention opinions which are opposed to my own, but I will do this in a general fashion, and, except in a few instances, without naming the particular authors. Specialists in the field will recognize them; as for others, my sole concern will be to furnish them with the reasons by which the positions which the tradition of the Church sets forth, are more solid than those to which I will be taking exception and which they will, unfortunately, often enough have the opportunity to read or to hear. I would like to prove to them that advances in modern scientific exegesis, in no way, call for "reinterpreting" the traditional teaching of the Church.

I would not have taken up my pen to write this book if it had not been for certain friends—priests, laity, religious, professors, catechists. I was responding verbally or in writing to questions which they had raised, regarding the difficulties which they were encountering and, in the process, came to the conclusion that writing this book was indeed a grave personal obligation binding in conscience. There is currently taking place in the Church something analogous to what happened during the third century of the Christian era, a phenomenon magnificently analyzed by Fr. Jules Lebreton of venerated memory; the lack of harmony between popular and scholarly theology.[4] Already, by this period, the speculations of scholars had been dangerously influenced by the scientific, philosophical, and cultural currents of the surrounding pagan world; and they often departed from the orthodoxy which the Christian population, guided by a sure spiritual instinct, more faithfully preserved. It is the same situation nowadays. "I bless you, Father, Lord of Heaven and of Earth, for hiding these things from the learned and the clever and revealing them to mere children" (Mt 11:25). No one can enter into the mystery of Jesus if he is not willing to become one of these children, these *népioï*, and if he does not consent to receive the faith of the Church from them. We may thank God that for a long time, throughout the history of the Church, there have been giants of intelligence who, at the same time, have been like these *népioï*; a St. Augustine, a St. Thomas, and so many others. And fortunately there are still many of them around today.

But the unsurpassed model of these little ones, is Mary, the Immaculate Virgin, the Mother of God. It is to her that I, filially, dedicate this book.

This book was not written with specialists in mind. That is why, in the text, itself, I have avoided every display of erudition which was not strictly necessary for understanding the point of view being set forth. But I do not wish to prevent specialists from reading my work and, at the opposite end of the spectrum, there are fortunately more and more well-educated members of the laity who want to apply as much seriousness and rigorous attention to reflecting upon the foundation of their faith as they apply in the area of their professional life.

With them in mind, I have relegated to footnotes whatever is needed to check the value of my assertions and, possibly, to pursue and deepen reflection on this question by further study.

If a reader finds himself hesitating before a technical expression, the meaning of which he does not fully understand, let him consult the short lexicon to be found at the conclusion of this work.

Introduction

QUESTIONS OF METHOD

1 The Historian's Point of View

It is certain that the question; Did Jesus think that he was God?[1] is, in itself, a question which has relevance for the historian. He can answer "affirmatively" without believing thereby in the divinity of Christ. In the same way he will answer affirmatively to the question: Was Mohammed convinced of being sent by God in order to transmit his word to men? But he will not necessarily share this conviction. In order to respond to the question which is posed in these words: Did Jesus think that he was God?—several ways are open to the historian.

The first, the one most often followed and one which leads to a negative response can be described in the following fashion: The image of the consciousness of Jesus presented by the Gospel of John is compared with that stemming from the earliest sources. These latter sources would have been obtained by historical critical methods presently accepted by modern exegesis. And although some will conclude that the sources are incompatible, still there is need to choose one over the other. The sound historical method necessarily tends toward choosing the earlier sources; but despite the considerable number of renowned exegetes who proceed in this fashion, it is important to observe that this approach has only the appearances of scientific rigor. It would be correct if it were based upon possible *contradictions*, in the strict and precise sense of the term, between John and his sources (one affirming what the other denies, and in the same way); but we do not find this here and with good cause. The approach which I am criticizing comes down to saying that a normal photograph and an X-ray photograph cannot represent the same person, or that the photograph of Mont Blanc viewed from Chamonix cannot represent the same reality as a photograph of the same mountain taken from Courmayeur.

However, a more rigorous scientific method does exist. It will consist in raising questions regarding the *cause* of these differences between the Johannine presentation and the most ancient sources with respect to the portrait which they offer us of the person of Jesus and of his self-awareness. Three hypotheses emerge: (1) a progressive discovery of the true dimension of the same historical person, Jesus of Nazareth; (2) a theological elaboration in John on the subject, not of Jesus of Nazareth, but of the Christ confessed by the faith of the Church of his time—an elaboration which he would have clothed with the literary form of a gospel of the life of Jesus; (3) the influence of doctrines issuing from various contemporary religious environments which would have deformed the Jesus of history as he was in reality.[2]

The historian cannot, a priori, exclude any of these possibilities. In the most careful way possible, he must weigh the pros and cons of each of these three possibilities. I believe that, even from the strictly historical point of view, the first hypothesis is the most solid. But as there does not exist a scale to allow a precise weighing of the pros and cons, the final judgment will be determined by the "precomprehension" of the historian, arising out of his own environment and his own options.*

---

*By way of parenthesis, let us explain what this precomprehension is: this word does not yet appear in dictionaries, but it is more and more coming to be used by exegetes, and it will be frequently mentioned in this book. It is a notion akin to that of *preconceived ideas* but does not include the pejorative aspect which is attached to this expression.

2 The Believer's Point of View

Since in every way the precomprehension arising out of the personal options of the historian plays an unavoidable and a determining role—a role presently recognized by practically all of those who reflect on the nature of historical knowledge[3]—would it not be better to start with this understanding from the beginning, even if, in a second step, we will critique it and call it into question again, if it appears contradicted by the *solid* data of the historical inquiry?

This is the method which I propose to follow in the present work. I will start with the faith of the community to which I belong, the Catholic Church.

When I read a particular text touching on a matter which has a certain importance for me, I necessarily already have some ideas on the matter, ideas stemming from my education, from my culture, from my opinions, etc. That this is so is normal; otherwise, this text would have no interest for me. This is what is called precomprehension. What at present is universally recognized is that this precomprehension colors my reading of the text and conditions my interpretation of it. I must obviously take this conditioning into consideration and eventually accept the fact that this text challenges my precomprehension and eventually modifies it.

Moreover, the further my cultural environment is removed from that of the text which I wish to understand (a distancing not only in time but also in mentality), the more I run the risk of reading this text with distorted spectacles which would warp my reading of the text. When it is a matter of major texts which are at the very beginning of a cultural religious movement, one of the best means for lessening this risk is to place oneself deliberately in one of the traditions stemming from this text.

But if, right at the outset, I want to place myself within the precomprehension stemming from my deepest convictions—that of the Catholic faith—it is important, first of all, to be aware of the critical and historical makeup of the content of my faith regarding the question at issue, not in order to discuss it or to take exception to it but rather in order to specify what it proposes that I should hold. If there were a decision of the solemn magisterium of the Church pronouncing on the question of the knowledge that Jesus had of his divinity (canon of an ecumenical council, infallible definition of the Pope), further discussion of this question would be authoritatively ruled out. Such an act of the magisterium does not exist. But my faith must likewise adhere to what the ordinary and universal magisterium, as an infallible interpreter of divine revelation teaches: that is to say, the unanimous teaching of pastors and theologians, authentic interpreters of the faith of the entire Christian people. We will see that such is indeed the case with respect to what is the object of our research. We will likewise see that, at a certain period, this faith was *decisively* manifested, that is to say, in response to a denial.

Hence the plan of the present study!

In the First Part, we will study the tradition of the Church and see that it is unanimous; Jesus was God and he knew it. And, as we will see, this tradition demands our acceptance by faith. The Second Part, titled—"The Jesus of History and the Jesus of the Historians"—will show that this conviction of faith is not opposed to that of the historian, faithful to rational but nonrationalistic methods. Certainly he will not be able to establish, with mathematical exactness, the historical truth of the faith of the Church; but, if he is faithful to the demands of his method, he must, at least, leave the question open. And he will have to recognize the value of the arguments which the Christian historian, true to the faith of his Church, will raise in order to root his conviction in a serious historical and critical inquiry. He will even be able to go further and speak about which side the balance of arguments for or against this affirmation of the Church is tilting.

Finally, a third part, titled "Faith of the Church and the Modern Mentality," will seek to set forth the weighty reasons for hesitation and even negation by many Christians today regarding the subject which we are considering: if Jesus knew that he was God, it is said, he would not really be sharing in our human condition. We hope to show the erroneous nature of such an understanding which, instead of being an authentic precomprehension, in the sense defined above, is a dangerous presumption.

The conclusion will be simple: There is no serious reason for ruling out knowledge of his own mystery on the part of the historical Jesus: the Son of God preexisting in glory from all eternity, true God and true Man. What the Church believed from the beginning and throughout twenty centuries, today's Christian is able and must continue to believe. The Jesus, presented by the Fourth Gospel, is the real Jesus of Nazareth such as he understood himself.

FIRST PART

Tradition

I

The Purpose of the Fourth Gospel

In this chapter, we will not be studying the historical value of the testimony of John's Gospel on the subject of this inquiry: Did Jesus know that he was God? We will treat this question in the Second Part. What we wish to examine here is the scope of the testimony itself, since it is upon this testimony that the traditional faith of the Church will be based. The question may be posed as follows: Does John believe and does he wish to have us believe that the person whom he is describing is the real Jesus of Nazareth such as he presented himself? Or rather does he wish to present us with a theological elaboration of the faith of the community in which he lived, a faith which, in order to be more easily assimilated, took the literary form of a gospel? In this latter case, the author and his readers or immediate hearers would have been perfectly aware of the process and the fictitious nature of the words and behavior attributed to Jesus. This process was actually in use at the time when the Fourth Gospel appeared: It is the literary genre of *midrash* in Jewish literature.

In this literary genre, words and actions totally anachronistic and actually reflecting convictions proper to the authors of the *midrash* are attributed to the major characters in Israel's history. But the reader or the hearer was not duped! This process is similarly used in certain biblical books: Jonas, Tobias, Esther, Judith. Closer to us, Sartre expressed his philosophical ideas by utilizing the form of historical novels, mixing reality and fiction, statesmen, real events, personalities, and situations deriving from the imagination of the author (the series, "The Paths of Liberty"). He obviously deceived no one.

The answer is crystal clear: John did not want to write a theological *midrash*. He wanted to present Jesus of Nazareth, his actions, his teachings, just as they really happened. It is certainly important to mention, right away, two further points which do not take away anything from what has just been said but which avoid more serious misunderstandings. On the one hand, John employs the freedom recognized by all historians of antiquity: They compose the *text* and the *circumstances* of the discourses which they attribute to the characters whom they are staging, but they claim to be expressing their ideas faithfully. Thus Caesar, in the *Gallic Wars,* has Vercingetorix speak like an accomplished Roman attorney, and in circumstances which are probable but about which the general would have been almost totally uninformed.

Moreover, the evangelist is convinced that the events of the death and the Resurrection of Jesus have allowed him a much better understanding of the meaning of Jesus' actions and teachings so that the Holy Spirit assisted him in understanding what he could not have been able to understand then (Jn 16:12-13); and that this same Spirit recalled to him the words of Jesus which he had forgotten (14-26).

But having admitted this, John is convinced that he is faithfully transmitting the message, the teaching, and the actions of the genuine Jesus of Nazareth in his historical reality. This is an essential point; how can it be established? By virtue of the purpose which he assigns to his Gospel in which he strives to convince precisely those who did not admit the divinity of Jesus.

Actually, by the first century, there were numerous *Christians* who denied the mystery of the Incarnation, that is to say, the divinity of Jesus, true God and true Man, especially among Christians who had come out of Judaism. They considered Jesus as the promised Messiah, the Messiah being merely a man, nothing more (such as the expectation of the entire Jewish people). We have very abundant evidence of such beliefs in the second and the third centuries of our era: in St. Justin, St. Irenaeus, St. Hippolytus.[1] But all scholars are in agreement in affirming that such a state of affairs can only be understood by virtue of being in continuity with a situation which would have had to have existed already in the first century. Moreover, we have very clear proofs that these ideas existed at the time in which the Fourth Gospel was written. The first two Epistles of St. John are irrefutable testimony. They characterize, as Antichrist, those who deny the reality of the Incarnation, which necessarily implies the denial of the divinity of Jesus of Nazareth (1 Jn 2:22-23; 4:2-3; 2 Jn 7).

But we have, most especially, the specific testimonies concerning the Fourth Gospel itself. According to St. Irenaeus, a disciple of St. Polycarp, himself a disciple of St. John, John wrote his Gospel in order to react against the heresy of Cerinthus and his disciples who denied the mystery of the Incarnation.[2] Similarly, St. Jerome affirms that St. John wrote his Gospel against the Ebionites who also considered Jesus a man.[3]

These testimonies, extrinsic to the Gospel, are confirmed by the very text of St. John: "There were many other signs that Jesus worked and the disciples saw, but they are not recorded in this book. These are recorded so that you may believe that Jesus is the Christ, the Son of God, and that believing this you may have life through his name" (Jn 20:30-31). This text, which has such great importance for our subject, demands that we linger over it. In these two sentences, the evangelist is indicating the purpose of his work: to show that Jesus is the Messiah and the Son of God. To show him to whom? To non-Christians (missionary preaching to Jews and pagans) or to Christians (catechetical instructions for the baptized in order to strengthen and defend their faith, perhaps disturbed by disputes coming from outside)? Exegetes are divided on this question. The most cautious response is certainly the one which refuses to choose: The Gospel is addressed to Christians and non-Christians, with a greater importance, however, accorded to the former, since the Gospel already presupposes knowledge of the elementary principles of the Christian faith. In what is of concern to us here, this problem is secondary: The same arguments which can lead non-Christians to faith can, by their very nature, strengthen the faith of the baptized disturbed by the objections of non-Christians and Christians moving away from the truth which St. John announces.

The signs mentioned in John 20:30, therefore, have a double purpose. To prove that Jesus is indeed the expected Messiah, a proof which is addressed to the Jews and Christians who are sensitive to Jewish objections; and to prove that Jesus is Son of God in order to convince those who deny him: Jews, pagans, Gnostic and Judaizing Christians, Christians impressed by their propaganda.

In what sense does the Gospel understand the expression Son of God in John 20:31? It is a question of a strict transcendent meaning regarding the divinity of Jesus which Thomas has just confessed (Jn 20:28). In this matter Lagrange, Schnakenburg, R.E. Brown, Barrett, Feuillet, and others are in agreement.

But it is here that the decisive argument is found which proves unquestionably that John really wanted to convince his audience that Jesus was truly God and that he was aware of it. By *themselves*, the signs could, if need be, establish that Jesus was the Messiah because he fulfilled the expected messianic signs (cf. Mt 11:4-5). But they were absolutely incapable of proving, by themselves alone, that Jesus was God, Son of God. So many miracles have been performed in the Bible by mere mortals who were sent by God! But they bear witness to the truth *of the teaching of Jesus regarding his divinity*.

The plan of the argument is clearly set forth by the first three evangelists in the episode regarding the cure of the paralytic (Mt 9:6 and parallels). "But to prove to you that the Son of Man has authority on earth to forgive sins—he said to the paralytic—"Get up, pick up your bed, and go off home."

We find exactly the same approach in the Fourth Gospel: "Believe me, I am in the Father and the Father is in me. At least, believe me for the very work's sake (King James)" (Jn 14:11).

But—and this is the central point of our argumentation—the miracles of Jesus witness to the truth of the teaching of this same Jesus. The miracles of Jesus cannot be used to prove the truth of the teaching of Paul, or of a dogma subsequently set forth by the believing community. In other words, St. John would be an impostor if he thought that Jesus had not taught his divinity and if he still wanted to have this divinity accepted by his readers by giving them the miracles that Jesus had performed as proof. Let us point out, at this particular stage of our work, that we are not yet supposing either the historical truth of the Fourth Gospel or the truth of the affirmation: Jesus of Nazareth was God and he was aware of it. We are positioning ourselves on the level of the intention and convictions of the evangelist: Either St. John is a bold-faced liar or he is convinced and wishes to convince his readers that Jesus did teach that he was God and that he proved this by his miracles.

Such an intention and conviction of the evangelist had additional relevance when we take into account the situation of the Christian world at the end of the first century. The divinity of Jesus was being contested, even denied by many, as we have just seen (cf. p. 11). In such a situation, even independently of the intention of the author clearly expressed in Chapter 20: 30-31, the Fourth Gospel totally assumes a polemical approach by taking such a clear position on a question which is so contested.

We thus see how necessary it is to nuance the statement of R. E. Brown in the work already cited[4]:

> The present writer believes strongly that there is a core of historical material in the Fourth Gospel, but he also recognizes that this material has been re-thought in the light of late first century theology. The Gospel was written to prove that Jesus is the Son of God (20:31), and the evangelist accomplishes this by letting Jesus speak as He is now in glory. The words may often be the words of Jesus of the ministry, but they are suffused with the glory of the risen Jesus.

That the words of Jesus in the Fourth Gospel have been made more explicit by the evangelist in the light of the

Resurrection, is altogether correct, and the Second Vatican Council strongly affirms this.[5] But, in the light of what has just been said, it is clear that John had the conviction of transmitting faithfully what Jesus taught during his earthly life: The words could change, the framework, also the circumstances, but the *substance* was identical. And, specifically, one of the essential characteristics of the Johannine message is the following: In his profound reality, Jesus was already essentially, during his earthly life, what he is now in Heaven. All commentators on the Fourth Gospel are in agreement on this point.[6] If the evangelist had not been convinced of it, if he had been persuaded that Jesus of Nazareth would not be able to recognize himself in the portrait which he had drawn, he would be nothing but a wretched imposter, since he would have wanted to convince his readers of what he himself knew to be false.[7]

But one final objection can be made, namely: Granted, the evangelist *was* convinced that the words and actions of Jesus of Nazareth were substantially faithful to historical reality; but isn't he deceiving himself and deceiving himself in good faith, precisely because of a lack of an historical sense?

At the point at which this inquiry has so far taken us, it is still not possible to answer this very important question. We will attempt to do so in the Second Part. It is sufficient for us at this moment to have established, on very solid grounds, the following point: *The author of the Fourth Gospel is convinced that the portrait that he drew of Jesus of Nazareth, of his deeds, of his words, is substantially conformed to historical reality: Jesus was God and he knew it. And if, in his turn, the evangelist knew it, he derived this knowledge from a unique source: the life, activities, teachings of the historical Jesus, more completely understood because of the Holy Spirit. And the evangelist writes in order to share his conviction with his readers.*

II

The Fathers of the Church

1 The First Five Centuries

In the fathers of the Church, we do not find discussions regarding the question which forms the object of this book: Did Jesus know that he was God? This question had no meaning for them. The fact that Jesus had really pronounced the words which the evangelists attribute to him, was, at that time, a conviction which was common to everyone, to the fathers of the Church and to their adversaries. Therefore the question: Did Jesus know that he was God was identical to this further question: Was Jesus God?—since the answer is in essence based on the very words of Jesus which everyone admitted as expressing what Jesus knew and revealed about his own mystery.

Yet, in some manner, we can come indirectly to the opinion of the fathers on this subject by examining their reactions regarding the problem of the *ignorance of Christ*, a problem widely debated in the course of Christian antiquity on the various levels of Christological controversies having to do with Arianism and Nestorianism. This is especially the case regarding the celebrated text of Mark 13:32 in which Jesus says that no one knows the day and hour of the Last Judgment, neither the angels, nor the Son, only the Father. Actually, this text quite quickly became a weapon in the hands of those who denied that Christ was truly God equal to the Father (Arians) or that Jesus and the Second Person of the Trinity are the same person (Nestorians).

15

What is interesting for our purpose is the following
evidence: Prior to this text's becoming a bone of contention
in the Christological controversies, there was no problem
with admitting the ignorance of Jesus: for example, in St.
Irenaeus and Origen.[1] But eventually the fundamental
preoccupation was not the obvious meaning of the text
but the concern for interpreting this ignorance in such a
fashion as not to cast aspersions or a slur on the divinity of
Christ. Jesus would have to have knowledge which corresponded to his mystery as God made Man. Whence the
two directions in the interpretations of this text: Jesus, even
as man, was not ignorant of the day of judgment but he
was ignorant of it insofar as one sent by God since this
knowledge does not form part of the realities that he had
the mission to reveal; this interpretation was by far the most
common[2] and it has been maintained even up to our own
day.[3] Or, then again, a second interpretation: Jesus insofar
as he was man was not aware of the date of the last day, but
insofar as he was God, he knew it. Jesus therefore spoke
in Mark 13:32 of what he was ignorant of by virtue of his
human knowledge.[4]

However, it is important to point out that, in both interpretations, the fathers were convinced that Jesus of Nazareth,
the son of Mary, had, at his disposal, both his human knowledge as Son of Man and his divine knowledge as Son of
God. It was not a matter, in this instance, of the results of a
philosophical anthropology which was Greek in origin (the
concepts of person and of nature). It was very simply fidelity
to the Gospel data which was the basis of this certitude.
When they read: "The Father and I are one" (Jn 10:30),
they were convinced that Jesus said that, not insofar as he
was Man, but according to his divine nature. This is what
Pope St. Leo the Great clearly set forth in his celebrated
Tome to Flavian (449) which had been hailed at the Council
of Chalcedon (451).[5]

On the other hand, the fathers did not seem to raise the
question of *how*. How could this divine knowledge be expressed in words, in human concepts produced by a human
intelligence? This question never surfaced. They restricted
themselves to affirming the *fact*. The eternal Son of the

Father and Jesus, son of Mary of Nazareth, are the same *person*. Therefore God, the *Verbum*, speaks through the mouth of Jesus by means of the humanity which he assumes. Even, in St. Augustine, the analysis is not pushed further beyond its limits.[6]

Consequently, we see that the question—Did Jesus know that he was God?—was, for the fathers, a matter devoid of any significance. In their eyes, it was quite similar to the following question: Did God know that he was God? It is at the end of the period which we are studying, in 553, that the first official document of the magisterium of the Church on the question of the knowledge of Christ appeared: It was a condemnation rendered by Pope Vigilius, at the request of the Byzantine Emperor Justinian, against the Nestorians:

> If anyone says that the one Jesus Christ who is both true Son of God and true Son of Man did not know the future or the day of the last judgment and that He could know only as much as the divinity, dwelling in Him as in another (person), revealed to Him, anathema sit.[7]

We certainly see what this text intended to affirm: Jesus knew everything because he is God. This knowledge is not the product of a revelation. Jesus, as man, possessed this divine knowledge by virtue of the unity of his divine person, God made Man. In other words, Jesus, as man, by virtue of his divine person, knew what God knew. We can therefore deduce from this: God knew that he is God, therefore Jesus likewise knew it.

This text is one hundred years after the Council of Chalcedon which affirmed the presence in Jesus Christ of two natures, human and divine, in their perfection, their distinction, and their proper operations. But the definitions of Chalcedon had not yet borne all of their fruits. A deeper reflection on the implications of the definitions of this Council necessitates pushing the analysis even further without sacrificing anything which has just been said, but by specifying and by distinguishing, even more, the different levels of knowledge.

2 St. Fulgentius

We have to wait until the beginning of the sixth century in order for the question which forms the object of this book to be set forth with precision. Around the year 500, St. Fulgentius, Bishop of Ruspe in North Africa, responded to a certain Ferrand, deacon of Carthage, who had posed the following question to him: Does the soul of Christ have full knowledge of the divinity which has assumed it? Does the Son, by his humanity, know his divinity in the same way as the Father, the Son, and the Holy Spirit are aware of one another.[8]

It will be remarked that the question is not exactly: Did Jesus know that he is God? But rather: Did Christ, in his humanity, have a *full* knowledge of his divinity? The stress is on the word: *full*, and the question continues: Is this knowledge identical to the knowledge which the divine persons had of one another?

Fulgentius responds *yes* to the first question and *no* to the second. The soul of Christ, since it was created, has a creaturely knowledge. God who is uncreated has a divine and infinite knowledge. Christ, in his humanity, knows everything that God knows but not with the same infinite depth; therefore, Jesus, according to his human knowledge, is fully aware of his divinity, but not with a fullness which is identical to that by which God is aware of himself by virtue of his divine intelligence identical with his divine nature.[9] However, St. Fulgentius boldly affirms that this divine knowledge is communicated to the humanity of Christ by the Spirit who is given to him unreservedly (according to Jn 3:34-35).[10] Therefore, Jesus, in his humanity, is aware of his divinity in its complete fullness, a fullness limited only by the creaturely status of the human nature of the Savior. The analysis is not being pushed farther back. But a great advance takes place with regard to St. Augustine. Between St. Augustine and St. Fulgentius, the Council of Chalcedon, which clearly affirmed the two natures of Christ, took place: "Perfect in His divinity, perfect in His humanity" (. . .), without confusion (. . .), the character proper to each of the two natures being preserved."[11] Consequently, the words and the actions of Jesus of Nazareth can no longer be *immediately* attributed to his divine nature; it is necessary that they be so by the intermediary of his human faculties. Jesus knew that he was God but this knowledge had its source immediately in his human intelligence. This has some very important consequences for the interpretation of Mark 13:32 on the lack of knowledge regarding the day of judgment. When the fathers say that Jesus, as God, knew this day; and that, as man, he was ignorant of it, they were convinced, and rightly so, that the divine knowledge of the *Verbum* was accessible to Jesus the man. The definitions of the Council of Chalcedon implied that this divine knowledge of the *Verbum* is, in one way or another, communicated to the human knowledge of the Son of Mary in order that he might use it. Consequently, we can no longer say that Jesus knew the day of judgment as God and that he was ignorant of it as man since if Jesus of Nazareth, the son of Mary, knew this day insofar as he is God, it was necessarily by means of his intelligence as man; thus even as man he had to know it. This Letter of St. Fulgentius had tremendous influence among subsequent Latin authors. Alcuin, contemporary of Charlemagne, drew a great deal of inspiration from it, as did Hugh of St. Victor (around 1120).[12]

3 The Agnoetes

It would have been nice to glean a number of valuable indications in the writings regarding the various opinions and notions of the *Agnoetes*. Designated by this name are those Christians who admitted a certain ignorance in Jesus (in Greek *agnoein*, to be ignorant). But our knowledge of these currents is very fragmentary[13] and it seems that we are dealing here with individuals and not with groups. The patristic literature regarding these questions extends between 540 and 640. It is always a matter of the same problems, principally that of Mark, 13:32 on the lack of knowledge regarding the day of judgment. The reaction of the fathers is clearer and more unanimous than in preceding centuries: even as man, Jesus was ignorant of nothing. We perceive the influence of the on-going question stemming from Chalcedon, which we have attempted to delineate in the preceding paragraph: if Jesus, by divine knowledge, knew the day of judgment, he would also have to know it by his human knowledge.

The most important text for our purposes is a letter of Pope St. Gregory the Great to the Patriarch of Alexandria regarding the *Agnoetes* (around 600). He makes a very profound, although apparently subtle, distinction as he himself recognizes: Jesus knew the day of judgment in his human nature but not from his human nature.[14] He means that this knowledge of the day of judgment is not the result of normal activity on the part of his human intelligence. It is the divine knowledge of the *Verbum* but communicated to the human intelligence of Jesus. Let us conclude by saying a word about St. John Damascene (675-749), one of the last authors to speak of the *Agnoetes*.[15] In his presentation of the Orthodox faith, he explicitly affirms that the human intelligence of Jesus, while operating fully according to its own proper human nature, was conscious of being the intelligence of a divine person and not that of a man who would only be a man.[16]

In conclusion, we observe that, at the end of the patristic period, two things are clearly affirmed: The fullness and the perfection of the humanity of Jesus, of his intelligence as man; and, at the same time, the consciousness that this intelligence possesses of being the intelligence of a divine person. This divine person communicates to his human intelligence, according to its created capacity, its properly divine knowledge. It remains for us to reflect on the how of this communication: Such will be the task of theologians of the Middle Ages and of modern times.

III

The Theologians

The role of theologians—those of the Middle Ages and those of modern times—is going to consist mainly in attempting to respond to the question which the fathers left unresolved: *How* is the divine knowledge of the *Verbum* communicated to the holy humanity of Christ? For the solution of this problem depends upon an adequate response to the question which forms the basis of this book. Indeed, we can only state with certitude: "Jesus knew that he was God" by responding to the question: "How did he know it"? and this response can only be given by enlarging the question in order to consider the entire mystery of the human knowledge of Jesus of Nazareth.

1 The Theologians of the Middle Ages

We have seen the fathers, by their fidelity to the data of the Gospels, unanimously affirm that Jesus of Nazareth, the son of Mary not only was the Son of God but even had fully, at his disposal, the divine knowledge and awareness that was proper to the Son of God. We have seen also that, in fidelity to the Council of Chalcedon, the fathers of the fifth and sixth centuries taught that this divine knowledge was expressed by the mouth of a man, by the behavior of a man, and in human concepts and ideas produced by a human intelligence. It was therefore important that this divine knowledge be in some way "conveyed" by means of a human intelligence. How? This is the question that the theologians of the Middle Ages sought to resolve.

After a certain number of hesitations over which there is no use in delaying,[1] the majority of theologians of the thirteenth century distinguished three levels in the human knowledge of Jesus[2]: the acquired knowledge which every man possesses; that which the elect in heaven possess: beatific vision, the face to face vision of God; and "infused" knowledge of the type by which prophets transmit divine revelation to men. This doctrinal elaboration is not, as is often thought, an a *priori* philosophical construction as a superficial reading of St. Thomas might lead us to suppose. It is imposed on theologians as the best way of taking account of the biblical evidence. That, like all men, Jesus possessed an acquired knowledge which developed with age, is stressed by Luke 2:52: Jesus grew in wisdom. With respect to the vision of God which the elect in heaven possess with total clarity, three texts of the Fourth Gospel imply this: John 1:18; 6:46; 8:38.[3]

Infused knowledge is linked, in a looser fashion, to the biblical text. Since Jesus is proclaimed, in the Gospel, a prophet (Mt 13:57; Lk 13:33), it is normal that he have, like the prophets, knowledge of that which he is charged to reveal to men. And by virtue of the eminent dignity of Christ, it is appropriate that this knowledge be permanent and not something fleeting as was the case with the messengers of God during the Old Testament period.[4]

Yet it is important not to forget how this theology came to be elaborated if we are to respond to the question which concerns us: Did Jesus know that he was God? And how?

Faithful to the teachings of the Council of Chalcedon, St. Thomas calmly affirms: If there were not in Christ a knowledge other than properly divine knowledge, he would not be able to know anything at all.[5] Knowledge is an act of the person of Christ, but acting with the faculties of his nature. The Jesus of the Gospels appears in his human nature and his words were the product of human intelligence. The Council of Chalcedon teaches that, in Jesus, both natures, divine and human, exist in a distinct manner without mixture or confusion. The divine intelligence of the Son of God, God himself, cannot therefore make up for the absence of a human intelligence in the Incarnate Word. Consequently, if Jesus knows that he is God, as St. John affirms, he can only know it by means of his human intelligence. How is that? For St. Thomas the response is clear: by means of the beatific vision, that which is enjoyed by the elect in heaven, and which Jesus possesses here on earth. Through this "knowledge of the beatific vision" he sees God, his unity, the Trinity of divine persons, and he sees himself united to the Second Person of the Trinity in the unity of one single person.[6] But what would happen if Christ did not possess this beatific vision here on earth, if he hadn't even this infused knowledge which belongs to the prophets,[7] and if he possessed only this "acquired knowledge" common to all men, without exception? Would Jesus have known that he was God? This question, which we are going to see momentarily, is explicitly formulated by modern theologians. Yet, St. Thomas never posed it for himself. We do not find any mention of it in the great classical commentaries on the Angelic Doctor: Cajetan, John of St. Thomas, the Carmelites of Salamanca, Gonet, Billuart. Nonetheless, the coherence in the thought of St. Thomas calls for the response which modern Thomists have given. This response is negative. We must now treat this issue.

2 Modern Theologians

It is only in the twentieth century that speculative theologians have posed the question: How did Jesus know that he was God? It is important to insist on the "how." Unlike certain modern exegetes and some theologians influenced by them, the authors whom we are going to survey quickly are absolutely convinced, by all of the tradition which precedes them, that Jesus had full knowledge of his mystery as God-Man. What they are investigating is the place of this knowledge in the anthropological constitution of Jesus-Man, in his human intelligence. Consequently, when they pose the question, Would Jesus know that he is God if he did not have knowledge derived from the beatific vision of the saints in heaven or the infused knowledge of the prophets, they are perfectly conscious of envisioning a theoretical state which never existed. It is the same matter when theologians speak of man in the state of pure nature without grace, which makes man a child of God, and without sin, which corrupts human nature. It is a state which has never existed but the consideration of which is indispensable for understanding much better what does exist: If we speak of human nature wounded by sin (the state of man after the fall), this wounding can be obviously understood only in relationship to a state in which wounding did not exist. Likewise in order to know where the knowledge which Jesus had of his own Mystery as God-Man is located, there is no other method than that which consists in envisaging in a theoretical and abstract fashion, what would happen if Christ did not possess the different levels of knowledge distinguished previously.

For certain modern theologians the knowledge which the man Jesus possessed regarding his divine nature was given to him straight off by the very fact of the hypostatic union, namely, the union in one single divine person of the divine nature and of the human nature.[8] But Thomistic theologians do not accept this solution which seems to revert to the "knowledge from union" of Alexander of Hales, explicitly rejected by St. Thomas.[9] The awareness that Jesus, as man, possessed of being a divine person can only derive from his human knowledge, according to one of the two elements of this knowledge which we have treated previously: knowledge from the beatific vision or infused knowledge. For acquired knowledge, common to all men, however perfect it may be, cannot go beyond the capacities of human nature as such. It is, some think,[10] through his infused knowledge (prophetic knowledge) that Jesus could derive his certitude of being God. By means of it, he possesses the revelation that he is God. But, for the majority of Thomistic theologians, it is by means of the knowledge of the beatific vision (that of the saints in heaven) that Jesus knows with certitude that he is true God and true Man.[11] Be that as it may, all these Thomistic theologians are in agreement on one point, which is very important for the problem which we are treating: If Jesus possessed merely acquired knowledge, that is to say the knowledge, common to all men, which is acquired by the normal exercise of intelligence given to every man in his human nature, in this case, Jesus would be God, but he would not know it.[12] Let us stress once again that we are dealing with an unreal hypothesis, recognized as such by those who frame it and who are all convinced that Jesus knew that he was God. An hypothesis bordering even upon absurdity, not metaphysical or ontological, yet with respect to the inner logic of the plan of God: what would be served by elevating a creature to such a degree of excellence if, intelligent and free, he knew nothing about it? But this hypothesis, as unreal and absurd as it may be, is nevertheless theologically useful since it permits a better *analysis* of the different elements of the mystery of the Incarnation.

What follows is the result of this analysis: The mystery of the Incarnation does not intrinsically imply, in its intimate structure, knowledge by Jesus of Nazareth about his divine nature. In other words, a Jesus who would be God but who would not know it does not imply any contradiction in the structure of the mystery of the God-Man; but it introduces a certain illogicality in the wisdom of the plan of God. Let us further observe that these authors who think in this way are not *avant-garde* theologians—far from it, they are faithful guardians of the tradition of the Church and of the thought of St. Thomas Aquinas. By way of summary then: With respect to the mystery of the Incarnation, the knowledge that Jesus possessed of his divinity represents a *supplement*, but a *necessary* supplement.

An important consequence flows from this: One can deny or cast in doubt the knowledge that Jesus possessed about his divinity without thereby ceasing to confess one's faith in the divinity of Christ. Naturally, such an attitude is very dangerous. In the following chapter, we are going to see why by demonstrating that the affirmation by which Jesus was perfectly aware that he was God is a doctrine which possesses all the required characteristics for being proclaimed a dogma of faith. But in any case it is a matter of an article of faith *distinct* from one which affirms the divinity of Jesus Christ.

IV

The Faith of the Church Affirms It: Jesus Knew that He Was God

We are now at the end of our study of statements from the Church's tradition.

By way of conclusion it is only proper to pose the question: What, according to the language of theologians, is the theological note of the statement: Jesus knew that he was God? Is it a dogma of faith like the divinity of Christ, or is it simply a theologically certain doctrine or even an opinion which can be freely discussed and debated?

In order to know if it is a dogma of faith, it is necessary to recall that the Church can explicitly recognize a truth of faith in two ways: in an extraordinary fashion by means of a dogmatic definition of the pope or of an ecumenical council; or, in an ordinary fashion, by what is called the ordinary universal magisterium of the Church, the habitual teaching of bishops in the normal exercise of their function as teachers in communion with the pope.[1] In neither case are we able to say that the pope and the bishops have taken a position on this point by virtue of the exercise of their teaching function (*magisterium*). But this ordinary or extraordinary magisterium does not function in an arbitrary fashion: It expresses the common faith of the Christian people, faith raised up and nourished by the Holy Spirit who guards, preserves, and develops the deposit of revelation confided by God to his Church. Therefore, prior to any declaration of the magisterium, a particular element of revelation is lived out and experienced by the Christian people as a reality in which they believe. A faith, often obscure and implicit, but which will be roused in response to questioning, to a denial. At the appropriate time, the role of the magisterium will be to give evidence for this faith and to verify the authentic nature of it (conformity with Scripture, tradition, liturgy, etc.)

Does this apply to what we are considering? We need to respond, Yes, unhesitatingly.

We have already seen how clearly evident it was for the majority of ordinary Christians: "If he is God, then clearly he knows it." Moreover the Fourth Gospel attests to it and, in the course of the life of the Church, as we have just explained, the fathers and the theologians have never cast doubt upon the fundamental historicity of Jesus' declarations regarding his divinity.

However, an objection does arise and it is a serious one: How many affirmations have been transmitted by unanimous tradition, attested to by Scripture, and finally abandoned in the wake of new certitudes stemming from advances in the various sciences! For example, the scientific exactness of the account in Genesis 1 on the creation of the world, the historicity of the book of Jonah, the attribution of chap. 40-66 of Isaiah to the author of the beginning of the book. . . .

Wouldn't this be quite similar to the problem being studied here? In fact, many exegetes and theologians think and say that the advances in exegesis and historical knowledge regarding Jesus of Nazareth compel the Church to exhibit the same attitude as it does regarding the subject matter of the opening chapter of Genesis.

Actually, we have, in this instance, a real problem: Many affirmations have been conveyed by the tradition of the Church in a noncritical fashion until such time as a dispute, due to advances in the sciences, challenges the Church which finally comes to the realization that these elements do not form part of Revelation. We have already given three examples of this. We could also mention pre-Copernican cosmology, Mosaic authenticity of the Pentateuch, and the author of the Second Epistle of Peter. . . .

These indisputable facts invite us to distinguish, in the tradition of the Church, between what is held in a *critical* fashion from what is transmitted in a *noncritical* fashion. At the very center of the difference we can locate the dispute which stems from a variety of causes and agents and which denies or casts doubt on the affirmations handed down by tradition. In the previously cited examples, after the passage of a certain amount of time and with some hesitation, the Church admitted the validity of the dispute. In other cases when faced with denial, the Church has firmly maintained its position: The dispute served to fortify, to firm up the faith of the Church regarding points about which their being called into question had value: the Real Presence of Christ in the Eucharist, original sin, the hierarchical structure of the Church. . . . In these latter cases, the Church, assisted by the Holy Spirit, understood well that the disputed points formed part of the deposit of faith which she was charged with preserving, transmitting, and teaching. In the first case, she likewise benefitted from the grace of the Holy Spirit, which allowed her to affirm that the dispute had no bearing upon the data of revelation. In any case, *never* in the history of the Church has there been a "coming and going" between the two categories; never has a declaration, proclaimed as forming part of the deposit of faith, eventually passed over into the category of pronouncements not bound up with the faith.

In which category are we to place the affirmation which is of interest to us: Jesus certainly knew he was God? Has there been a period in the life of the Church in which this affirmation has been held and maintained in a critical fashion in opposition to those who deny it? The answer is in the affirmative. The period of the Church's life when a similar dispute took place is in the apostolic period; and the text in which the Church affirmed its conviction has an infinitely greater force than a conciliar text, since it is an inspired biblical text—the Fourth Gospel.

This has been already shown in great detail in Chapter I, the conclusions of which we are now going to summarize.

In order to deal with those who deny the mystery of the Incarnation, John wrote his Gospel to show that Jesus is Son of God, God himself, and that this conviction has its source in the teaching of Jesus himself, whose truth is

attested to by miracles, the "signs," the "works" which
Jesus performed.

Two points are then affirmed in a critical fashion, that
is to say, in order to respond to denials and disputes,

> Jesus is Son of God, God himself.
> How do we know this? Because Jesus taught it.

Thus, by these two points, we see that if the knowledge
that Jesus had regarding his divinity is not directly affirmed
in the Fourth Gospel, it immediately follows from the
second point: the teaching of Jesus. This teaching, from all
evidence, has its basis in knowledge. This is a truism.

If we compare the knowledge that Jesus had of his divinity
with other truths of faith such as original sin, the Real
Presence of Christ in the Eucharist, for example, we immediately see what is similar and what is different. What
is similar? In both cases there is an affirmation of the faith
of the people of God when faced with a dispute, with a
denial. What is different? In the dogmas which have just
been mentioned, the phenomenon of dispute and the
affirmation of faith took place later on, in the course of the
life of the Church, by means of Councils solemnly reaffirm-
ing what was being questioned. As for the matter which
concerns us, this took place right at the very beginning,
during the course of the apostolic period, in a text which
forms part of Revelation, which is the Word of God.

Then, for nearly twenty centuries, this doctrine had
never been disputed, with no one casting doubt upon the
historicity of the teachings of Jesus as reported by St. John.
Of course, some modern theologians of irreproachable
orthodoxy have been able to distinguish the mystery of
the Incarnation and Jesus' knowledge of his divinity by
means of his human intelligence; and they have specified
that the former does not ontologically include the latter.
But they have always very strongly affirmed both.

The conclusion becomes clear. The affirmation that
Jesus knew that he was God forms part of the deposit of
the Church's faith. Certainly, it has not been defined by
the solemn and infallible magisterium of the Church, but

it fulfills all the necessary conditions for such a definition to be possible. With respect to the question which concerns us, the situation is quite similar to the situation in which the dogmas proclaimed in 1854, 1870, and 1950 found themselves prior to their definition by the Church: namely, the Immaculate Conception, Papal Infallibility, and the Assumption. These definitions created nothing new: They merely solemnly affirmed what was already believed by the Christian people as a whole.

At this time, it is important for us to show, in a second section of this book, how this faith of the Church stands in relationship to the work of the historian examining *biblical texts* and the *reality* of which these texts are witnesses.

The historian, in his method, uses only rational working tools; but he is not, for all of that, a rationalist, that is to say, one who excludes the supernatural, especially when he studies texts in which it is constantly a question of this suprarational reality. If he is faithful to his method, he should be able to compare the affirmation of the Church's tradition with what the study of the texts, examined in a critical fashion, reveal to him. We will see that he will have to conclude that these affirmations depend upon solid data, upon arguments which are valid because of sound historical methodology.

Let us recall what has already been said. *In itself*, this question concerns the competence of the historian. No one will deny that the historian has the right to ask himself the question: Did Alexander the Great consider himself to be God? The domain of Christian faith is not a forbidden zone surrounded by barbed wire and off limits to historical inquiry. But this historical inquiry must be conscious of its limitations and clearly exhibit the degree of certitude or uncertitude with respect to its results.

SECOND PART

The Jesus of History
and
the Jesus
of the Historians

V

A Working Hypothesis

This Second Part is attempting to compare, on the one hand, the faith of the Church, which the preceding chapters have set forth as evidence, and, on the other hand, the results of an historical, scientific, honest, exact, rational, but nonrationalistic inquiry.

In order to do this, we will use a method which is very rarely employed in biblical studies but which is of indisputable scientific rigor; it is very close to that method which we must have used to resolve problems in geometry during our high school and college days and the solution of which began with these words: "Given the following theorem to be proved." This method also belongs to the method which allowed the French astronomer, Le Verrier, to discover the planet Neptune; he presented a working hypothesis: the irregularities in the movement of planets were caused by the disturbing influence of an unknown planet. He situated this planet in the vault of the heavens ("given the following theorem to be proved"). And he calculated the position and the dimensions of the planet in such a way that it produced the same disturbances as those that he had observed. And we know that this planet had been discovered exactly in the place calculated for its presence.

Having said this, what follows is our working hypothesis: The various texts of the New Testament which speak of the mystery of Christ, of his preexistence, and his divinity are explained in the following fashion: *Jesus had the certitude of being God, Son of God. Everything which the New Testament said on this subject corresponds to what Jesus thought about himself and he manifested this conviction by his teaching and actions.*[1]

The legitimacy, better still, the accuracy of this working hypothesis will be established in the following fashion:

1. We will show how, in some sort of a priori fashion, Jesus was obliged to proceed in order to communicate his conviction to his disciples.

2. We will show the exact correspondence between the manner in which Jesus necessarily had to proceed—established a priori—and what the gospel and New Testament tradition—considered in its historical development—reveals to us.

Let us further clarify this working hypothesis. When I say Mohammed knew that he was sent by God, I am implying that he really was (objective level); when I say: Mohammed had the certitude of being sent by God, I can, quite properly, myself, not share this certitude and think that Mohammed had deceived himself (subjective level).

That is why our working hypothesis has been formulated in terms of subjective conviction (Jesus had the certitude of being God) and not of objective knowledge (Jesus knew that he was God). We are sticking closely to the domain which is proper to the historian who cannot affirm the divinity of Christ (a step which depends on faith), but who can, for Jesus, as for Mohammed, Alexander, Buddha, etc., ask himself about what *he himself* thought of his person and of his relationship with God.

1 Obstacles to the Revelation of the Mystery of Christ

After having formulated this working hypothesis, let us try now to reflect upon the conditions for revelation to man of this mystery. First of all, if we take into consideration the mentality of the closest disciples of Jesus, the revelation of this mystery runs up against a triple obstacle:

a. A religious mentality which would consider that what

is essential was obedience to the law of God promulgated by Moses, and which was hardly accustomed and hardly inclined to reflect upon God and his nature—a reflection considered by many as without profit, impossible, and sacrilegious.

b. A religious mentality fashioned out of confrontation with the idolatry all around it and for which anything which did not entirely square with the profession of the mono-theistic faith of Deuteronomy 6:4 was straight off considered idolatrous.

c. A religious mentality structured by eschatological and even apocalyptical thought: certitude that the end of everything was at hand, an enlivened expectation of this end which will see, at long last, the triumph of God over the enemies of Israel, as well as the good fortune and the glory of the people of God who will conquer those who have conquered it; an expectation which is even to be seen among the disciples after the Resurrection (cf. Acts 1:6).

It is certainly clear that when faced with a similar situation, the revelation of the mystery of God and of Christ could only be very progressive. In its beginning stages, only what squared with the religious mentality of the earliest disciples could be assimilated: Jesus prophet, legate of God; on the other hand, the divinity of Jesus could only be revealed to the disciples by behavior in which he assumed a power reserved to God alone ("your sins are forgiven you") and not by explicit declarations which could only give rise to indignant rejection.

Moreover, Jesus had to run the inevitable risk of allowing his words and actions to be interpreted on the basis of the mentality of his disciples, a mentality which, without neces-sarily falsifying the meaning of what they had seen and heard, would act in the manner of filtered glass, coloring or distorting, enlarging or diminishing to suit the situation, retaining or forgetting on the basis of whether or not what they had seen or heard conformed to their mentality, and finally coloring the words and actions of Jesus with foreign elements borrowed from their own religious horizon. It is evident that the greater the distance there is between what

Jesus said and did and what the disciples expected of him, the more likely the disciples were inclined to reduce, to forget, to color, or to distort.

Let us make an additional comment in this particular regard: In the working hypothesis set forth above, Jesus was convinced that he was God but he did not identify himself with God his Father, as the biblical texts clearly show. Moreover, he unhesitatingly and resolutely professed the absolute monotheism of the faith of Israel (cf. Dt 6:4, cited by Jesus in Mk 12:29). In the framework of our working hypothesis, Jesus would have the conception regarding his person, which is derived from the Johannine writings: He is God, his Father is God, and yet there is only one God. However, if formulating such a doctrine is still very difficult after twenty centuries of Christian existence and theological and dogmatic discussions, all the more reason for it to be, at the very beginning, almost impossible to arrive at a satisfactory formulation! There existed a tremendous risk of engendering an exaggerated polytheism, resembling those which the Bible reacted against with such relentless force. Jesus, therefore, had to take great pains to avoid provoking, in the mind of his faithful, one of the three errors which constitute the permanent temptation of the Christian: Jesus is not truly God; he isn't truly man; there are several Gods. And we notice right away the inescapable nature of a first stage in which Jesus would manifest the one who he was certain of being by actions rather than by words, by a manner of acting which would be tantamount to laying claim to divine attributes rather than by an explicit declaration which is almost inevitably a source of errors.

2 Three Stages

Whether from the perspective of the teaching and its intrinsic difficulty, or from the perspective of the disciples and their limited faculties of assimilation, everything points to a very progressive teaching. This progressive teaching can, a priori, be set forth in three stages.

In the first stage, concerning his person and his teaching, Jesus will not reveal everything which could be understood, but everything which could be accepted and assimilated without mistakes—given the prevailing mentality. But he will have to attempt to bring about an evolution in this mentality by demonstrating its narrow limits and eventual deviations.

A second stage will be centered on the formation of a group of disciples. Those attracted and won over by the teaching and the personality of the Master will have a favorable disposition which will allow them eventually to accept a teaching which goes beyond them and which shocks them and concerning all the dimensions of which they are still incapable of understanding.

A third stage will consist in making a selection from within this group of disciples in order to choose those privileged disciples to whom a higher doctrine will be able to be confided so that it may be announced to others when their own minds have received sufficient formation. It is important to insist upon the fact that these three stages can be supposed, a priori, by anyone totally ignorant of the gospel tradition. We will certainly be reproached for this schema's presenting, as a priori, what is in fact only a posteriori, and for saying that, in reality, it is the gospel tradition which is at the root of this distinction regarding the three stages.

We can respond that this schema totally squares with what history and the sociology of religions have to say about the evolution of religions, especially, regarding the relations between the founder, his disciples, and a wider audience.

VI

Historical Study of the Gospel Tradition

The first two stages:
The teaching of Jesus to the crowds and to the disciples

There can be no question here of refashioning the work of exegetes and of examining, under a critical angle, all the texts which speak to us of the consciousness that Jesus had of himself. We will restrict ourselves merely to registering the consensus of exegetes when and wherever it exists. When this consensus does not exist, and when it is difficult to discern a majority tendency, we will adopt the solution which appears to be based upon the best arguments.

1 The first stage: the public teaching of Jesus.

Let us attempt to gather together the elements of the primitive tradition, that is to say, the behavior and the words which, according to the majority of critics, emanate from Jesus himself during his public ministry (as opposed to the ministry which is geared to the disciples alone).

a Jesus the blasphemer

We would like to draw attention here to a point which is hardly contested: It seems that, according to the most primitive tradition, Jesus had been accused of blasphemy by his contemporaries because he usurped prerogatives which belonged to God alone.

This is recognized by the great majority of contemporary exegetes. On the occasion of the appearance of Jesus before the Jewish authorities, the accusation of blasphemy is explicitly set forth in Matthew 26:65; Mark 14:64; implicitly

in Luke 22:71, and John 19:7. Of course, exegetes are divided
on the nature of the accusation of blasphemy made against
Jesus, and even on the historicity of the dialogue between
Jesus and the high priest, given the different forms that it
takes among the various evangelists (and its absence in St.
John). This scepticism appears to me unjustified but has
no relevance here. A lesser charge cannot be seriously
entertained: The accusation of blasphemy "undeniably
re-echoes the manner in which the early Christians put
this at the head of the list of grievances brought against
Jesus."[1] But these early Christians were so very close to the
events of the earthly life of Jesus—only a few years separated
them from the death of the Lord—that we are, therefore, all
but certain that the accusations were real. What blasphemies
were at issue here? Certainly not those mentioned in rabbinic
tradition: To pronounce the name of Yahweh, to utter in
public an expression like the following: "Cursed be God."
Eliminating these two types of blasphemy, there remains
nothing except that which consists in laying claim to divine
prerogatives. A good example of this type of accusation is
given to us in Mark 2:7 (and the parallels in Matthew 9:3
and Luke 5:21): "How can this man talk like that? He is
blaspheming: Who can forgive sins but God"?[2] (see also
John 5:18; 10:33).

It is important to remark that, in the Bible, the apocrypha,
ancient Jewish literature, and rabbinic writings, no person,
belonging to the Jewish people, is accused of usurping
divine prerogatives. The sole examples of this are pagan
kings who wanted to be adored (Dn 3:1-7; 6:7-9; cf. Ez 28:2;
2Mc 9:12, etc.). We are, therefore, in the presence of something unique. Such an accusation, which is found nowhere
else, can only have a single basis or source: the behavior
of Jesus which would give rise to a similar charge.

b Jesus the legislator

Running like a refrain throughout the Sermon on the
Mount is the formula: "It has been said . . . but, I say to you"
(Mt 5:21, 27, 31, 33, 38). This formula introduces a modifica-
tion of the law of Moses in the direction of a greater demand.
We likewise find a similar tendency in Judaism. For example,

prohibition of divorce given by Jesus can be compared with the prohibition against polygamy made by rabbis in the tenth century of our era, even though both were explicitly permitted by the law of Moses. But what is unique and proper to Jesus is the formula employed by him: "It has been said ... but I say to you," the formula which has no parallel in the Old Testament or in Judaism. Even if, as it is important to stress, Jesus is not going contrary to the law of Moses but calling for people to go much further in the same direction, there is something unheard of here. Jesus, unlike Moses in Deuteronomy 6:1, doesn't say "Here are the commandments, the laws and the ordinances which the Lord, your God, has ordered to be taught to you." Unlike the prophets, he does not say: "Thus speaks the Lord, your God," but he simply affirms: "But I say to you." And we are dealing in this instance with an absolutely authentic word of Jesus: Almost everyone admits it.[3] "Jesus sovereignly enjoins the law and tradition, which he interprets, deepens and even corrects."[4] He thereby equates himself with God as Law-Giver.[5]

From this same perspective, another statement of Jesus must be taken into consideration: "He who loves his father or his mother more than me is not worthy of me" (Mt 10:37). Here again, the majority of critics believe they are capable of discerning an authentic statement of Jesus, if not in its form, at least in its content.[6] Once more, we have a statement without any real parallel either in the Bible or in Judaism.[7] And justifiably so: Who can demand that he be preferred over one's parents and children if not God alone?

c Jesus, the Son of God

Only once did Jesus designate himself Son of God in his public teaching, at least if we limit ourselves to texts which the majority of critics consider as transmitting words of the historical Jesus. It concerns, in this instance, the parable of the wicked husbandmen (Mk 12:6-8; cf. Mt 21:37-39; Lk 20:13-15). Here also, the great majority of modern exegetes recognize that this parable, in its nucleus, refers back to Jesus himself (especially the mention of the Son). Nevertheless, they tend to admit an important redactional working of the primitive Christian tradition, which does not touch upon the points which interest us here.[8] In this parable, we remember, a man plants a vineyard and rents it out to some husbandmen who mistreat or kill the servant whom he sends to them to collect the produce of the vineyard. "He had still someone left: his beloved son" (Mk 12:6). He sends him to them and they in turn kill him. As practically all the commentators remark, the allegory is clear. The owner is God, the servants are the prophets, the son is Jesus.[9]

Therefore, Jesus presents himself here clearly as the Son of God, by distinguishing himself from the prophets who are only servants. And at the same time this light which is too bright for his audience is, as it were, filtered by the literary genre of the parable which keeps the exact correspondence between the allegory and the reality from being explicitly set forth. Yet, for "one who has ears to hear" (cf. Mk 4:9), the lesson is clear. Fr. Leon-Dufour formulates it correctly: "What he (Jesus) says of himself concerns not only his mission but his person. Doesn't the figure of the son in the parable suggest that he is aware of being the Son of God"?[10] Now, then, given the mentality of his listeners, could Jesus have done more? In the preceding chapter, we have already shown that this was absolutely impossible (cf. above, p. 36).

We can, therefore, summarize as follows: When he spoke to an audience that encompassed more than just his disciples, Jesus insinuated that he was greater than all those who, prior to him, had been messengers of divine revelation. Moreover, he discreetly showed that he had a unique proximity to God, a connection that was incomparably superior to that of the legates of God in the past: These are the servants, he is the Son. He has clearly shown that he is exercising a power that belongs to God alone: legislative power, power of forgiving sins. His audience had understood correctly. They are the very ones who had accused him of blasphemy.

In order to be faithful to the historical-critical method adopted in this chapter, we will say nothing more about this question. We will simply add that the examined words of Jesus are open affirmations susceptible to yielding a

deeper meaning. Their content is not exhausted by a pre-
liminary, superficial understanding.

2 The second stage: Jesus' teaching to his disciples

Usually, the evangelists clearly distinguish between
the teachings of Jesus to the crowds and those addressed
to various groups of disciples. They even have a tendency
to group together teachings which had become scattered
in the course of time in order to form a set of discourses
issuing from a single source, addressed to one or the other
audience. Thus, in St. Matthew, the Sermon on the Mount
(chap. 5-7), and the parabolic discourse (chap. 13) have
the crowds for an audience: The missionary discourse
(chap. 10) and the discourse concerning the end of the
world (chap. 24-25) are addressed exclusively to the
disciples. In the Gospels we often find expressions such
as "He spoke to the crowds," "He spoke to the disciples,"
"Summoning the crowd at the same time as the disciples,"
or similar expressions (cf. Mt 11:7; Mk 7:14; Lk 5:3; 7:9,
etc.; Mt 9:37; 10:1; 15:32, etc.; Mk 8:34). Even if these nota-
tions sometimes convey a theological intention of the
evangelist (compare for example Mk 8:34 with Mt 16:24),
no one takes exception to the distinction between these
two types of teaching. In the early part of his ministry,
especially in Galilee, Jesus addressed himself above all to
the crowds. Finally when these crowds separated themselves little by little from him, he devoted his teaching
principally to the formation of his disciples.

But Jesus explicitly reveals much more to his disciples
regarding who he is: He reveals himself as the Son, the
one who calls God "Abba," that is to say "Papa or Daddy."

a Jesus, the Son of God

Two texts will be examined here because a great number
of critics see in them the authentic words of Jesus: Mark
13:32 (Mt 24:36) and Matthew 11:25-27 (Lk 10:21-22).

Having said this we do not wish to say that there do not
exist other texts (besides those just mentioned): for example
the confession of Peter, solemnly confirmed by Jesus: "You
are the Christ, the Son of the Living God" (Mt 16:16). I am

convinced that these words reflect the historical reality; but since the question is being debated for apparently serious reasons (the absence of "Son of the Living God" in the parallel texts of Mark and Luke), this text and others will be set aside for purposes of method (cf. p. 41).

Mk 13:32 and Mt 24:36.

This text deals with lack of knowledge regarding judgment day, already mentioned (p. 15), within Jesus' discourse about the end of time, a discourse addressed to the disciples exclusively (cf. Mk 13:3; Mt 24:3: "in particular") "But for that day or hour, nobody knows it, neither the angels in heaven, nor the Son, no one but the Father." In this case, exegetes, who admit that Jesus did indeed utter this sentence, are in the overwhelming majority. And the argument in favor of authenticity is very difficult to refute: Why would the community have invented a statement of Jesus at a time when it would ordinarily create a difficulty, since to admit this limitation of the knowledge of Christ would have been ill-advised and counterproductive. This statement could only come to find its way into the Gospel because it had actually been spoken. The fact that Luke omits it and that numerous manuscripts of Matthew suppress that part of the sentence concerning the lack of knowledge of the Son— all of this shows that this statement very soon encountered difficulty and, therefore, makes it altogether improbable that it had been invented at this moment.

Also a certain number of exegetes, impressed by this argument, hold for the sentence's being the word of Jesus. They add that the mere mention of the Father and of the Son is a reworking by the primitive community, thereby giving expression to its own theology of Christ. The weakness of this position is immediately evident. It is to decide, a priori, that Jesus could not use this word "Son," for no other argument is presented in place of it. These exegetes form only a small minority.

Later on, we will treat the exegetical problem of the lack of knowledge of the day of judgment by Jesus (cf. p. 15). What we wish to state here is that, at the very moment, when Jesus was instructing about his lack of knowledge,

he presents himself as "the Son," and God as "the Father."
On the other hand, we have a clear example of a crescendo:
the angels in heaven, the Son, the Father. The Son is, therefore, above the angels. Certainly it is a mistake to exaggerate
the significance of this gradation: Numerous rabbinic texts
actually present the Messiah and even the Just as superior
to the angels.[11] What is more important is the mention of
the angels *in heaven.*

The Son is, therefore, mentioned in between two heavenly
beings: the angels and the Father. In this way Jesus *insinuates*
that He is himself also a heavenly being. On the other hand,
the *paired* mention of the Father and of the Son also provides
food for thought. Father and Son are two correlative realities
in which one implies the other. Without being able to speak
of equality (in himself the Father is always superior) we
can, without going beyond the level of suggestion, detect
a sphere of common existence.

As we see it, it is not a matter of boldly stated affirmations,
without possible equivocation, but rather of insinuations.
Moreover, they are encased in a sentence the purpose of
which is, in no way, to set forth the exceptional grandeur
of the Christ but to stress and emphasize the impenetrable
mystery which surrounds the precise date of the final day,
a mystery known by the Father alone. Would an invention
by the Christian community, during the time of the clear
statements of St. Paul, have been all that discrete and clear
in its allusion?

Mt 11:25-27; Lk 10:21-22.

"I bless you, Father, Lord of heaven and of earth, for
hiding these things from the learned and the clever and
revealing them to mere children. Yes, Father, for that is
what it pleased you to do. Everything has been entrusted
to me by my Father; and no one knows the Son except the
Father, just as no one knows the Father except the Son and
those to whom the Son chooses to reveal him."[12]

The gospel context indicates less clearly than the pre-
ceding text that only the disciples heard this confidence.
The context is very uncertain in Matthew, more defined in
Luke, in which our passage is enclosed by two others

addressed to the disciples. But this consideration does not have great merit. What is more decisive is the very character of the words of Jesus, which, by their nature, appear to be incompatible with a discourse addressed to the crowds and which presuppose a certain degree of intimacy.

Regarding the difference of the preceding texts, we cannot say that the great majority of commentators attribute these verses to the historical Jesus; the opinion of the critics is strongly divided and there are some renowned exegetes on both sides of the question.[13] But what is very astonishing is the weakness of the arguments of those who do not accept our seeing an authentic statement of Jesus in this verse. As the author of a recent and very detailed study on this question has shown,[14] the arguments against the authenticity have all been laid low by recent research. The couplet "Father-Son" to speak of God and of man is attested to neither in contemporary Hellenism nor in Judaism so that it may be a Semitic expression or an expression of the Greek language. "Henceforth, it is not stupid to envisage here the influence of a vocabulary which is characteristic of Jesus, who, in the words of the gospel tradition, speaks of God, addresses himself to him and teaches his disciples the way to pray to him, by giving him the name of Father, Abba."[15] It couldn't have been put better. Let us go even further. From the explanations of this exegete we see that not only "is it not stupid," but it is much less so than the other explanations which have been set forth.[16] Thus, given the lack of weighty arguments on the other side and in accordance with the principles set forth above (p. 41), it is only fitting to regard Matthew 11:27 as an authentic statement of Jesus.

What relevance does it have for the subject which we are studying?

First of all there is everything which has been previously said regarding Mark 13:32 with reference to the Father-Son relation (above pp. 46-47).

But our text goes further than the passage previously studied and it does so in two respects:

(1) Jesus claims to have a knowledge of the Father, which

is comparably superior to that of other men. Human knowledge is, in reality, a nonknowledge when it is compared with that of Christ. In this instance, we have a declaration which is without parallel in the Bible, in Judaism and Hellenism.[17] No man ever claimed to be the only one to have knowledge of God.

(2) Similarly, God is the only one to know the true personality of Jesus. This implies that in Jesus of Nazareth there is a mystery known solely by God. Here again, we are in the presence of a declaration without precedent. As S. Legasse declares: "The idea which most naturally flows from the text is that there is a mystery of the Son, as there is a mystery of the Father. Only the Father knows the former, only the Son knows the latter along with those to whom he chooses to reveal it."[18] This formulation is all the more interesting in that it is the work of an exegete who carefully guards against unduly exaggerating the relevance of texts. But he very clearly and resolutely puts forth the reciprocity in the knowledge of the mystery of the Father by the Son and the mystery of the Son by the Father. Of course, nothing is said of the preexistence or of the divinity of the Son and the distance between the creature and creator can still perfectly exist as in the very close parallel of St. John 10:14: "I know my sheep and my sheep know me just as the Father knows me and I know the Father." The fact remains that the *text* is suggesting something as an equality, at least in a certain area, that of knowledge in the Semitic sense of the word, which signifies both knowing and loving in a totally indissoluble fashion. And this extends quite far: The Father knows the Son perfectly, totally, since he is God. From this it follows that the Son also knows the Father, totally and perfectly but who can perfectly know the Father if it is not God himself? Thus once again, all of this is not formally stated, and we can stick to a much more restricted meaning. But the text is *open*, admitting of more or less and even suggesting meanings of infinite depth.

b Abba

Jesus used to call God "Abba," that is to say very simply "Papa," "Daddy." In this instance, it is a matter *of speaking*

of God in a unique fashion without any parallel. Never was
God addressed by the title "Abba." This fact was solidly
established by recent exegesis[19] and is today *seriously* contested by no one. The word is found only once in the Gospel,
in the prayer of Jesus in the Garden of Gethsemane (Mk
14:36). We find it again in the prayer of Christians, called
to participate in the unique relation of the Son with his
Father (Rm 8:15; Gal 4:6). But if the Aramaic word, Abba,
is found in only one place in the Gospel, we can find it
again with certainty in other prayers of Jesus in which the
Greek word *Pater* correctly translates the Aramaic expression Abba: Matthew 11:25-26; Luke 23:34, 46, and probably
also the Lucan version of the Our Father (Lk 11:2).

What is the relevance of this invocation for the subject
which we are considering? It expresses, at the minimum,
an extremely close relationship of love between Jesus and
his Father, a familiarity which allows the absolute contrast
between the contemporary Jewish attitude and that of Jesus
in his invocation of the heavenly Father[20] to stand out clearly.
At the maximum, we see here, at least, an insinuation of a
certain equality between the Father and the Son.[21] And,
then again, it is important to state, as we have done previously, that it is impossible to make razor sharp distinctions
between these two interpretations. It is appropriate to
permit this invocation, Abba, to possess its own depth,
richness, and, above all, its own mystery.

We can now conclude this study of the words of Jesus
addressed solely to the disciples and revealing to them the
mystery of his relationship with the Father.

● Jesus shows himself as possessing a unique relationship of intimacy with and proximity to God.
● This intimacy places Jesus above the angels of heaven,
and it situates him as a heavenly being at the same time
as being an earthly being.
● Jesus knows the Father as the Father knows the Son;
in this there is the insinuation that, since, by nature, the
Father perfectly knows Jesus, therefore Jesus perfectly
knows the Father. It places him above all creatures who

can only imperfectly know the creator.

● Finally the title "Abba" suggests that there exists between Jesus and his Father an intimacy which has no analogy in the relationship of men with God, however special and privileged they may be.

VII

Historical Study of the Gospel Tradition (Conclusion)

The Third Stage: The Teaching of Jesus to His Privileged Disciples

Given the means which are at the disposal of the historian, we find ourselves here in an area which is much more difficult to explore: the origin of New Testament affirmations regarding the preexistence and the divinity of Jesus. In this section we want to establish that the belief of the primitive Christian community regarding the preexistence and the divinity of Jesus very probably took its origin from a teaching of Jesus presented to a limited circle of disciples. This is plausible and, from the historical point of view, extremely likely.

This affirmation is not new. Let us mention some of the better known exegetes who hold it: Fr. Lagrange, Oscar Cullmann, and H. Riesenfeld.[1]

The arguments which form the basis of this conviction will be grouped together in three sections: (1) The extremely rapid appearance, after Easter, of the doctrine of preexistence and of the divinity of Christ and the problem which this poses; (2) A negative argument: the unlikelihood of these doctrines being invented by the community; (3) A positive argument: indications of a teaching of Jesus to his disciples in this area.

1 The appearance after Easter of the doctrine of preexistence and the divinity of Jesus.

a Divinity of Christ

In this instance we are facing a fact that is uncontested

and recognized by all exegetes. Almost immediately after
Easter, in the bosom of the early Christian community, the
attitude of the faithful regarding the Risen Jesus is absolutely
identical with that of the believing Jew with respect to
Yahweh. Christians are those who invoke the name of
Lord (Kyrios) and "the name of the Lord is applied no
longer to Yahweh but to Jesus"[2] (Acts 2:21). One converts
to the Lord Jesus as one converts to Yahweh in the Old
Testament: Acts 9:35; 11:21. One believes in Jesus as one
believes in God: Acts 3:16. The Philippian hymn of 2:6-11
deserves special mention. Currently the majority of exegetes
think that Paul is quoting a Christian hymn which was
already known by his readers.[3] Similarly, today the great
majority of critics think that the Epistle to the Philippians
is contemporaneous with the major Pauline Epistles (around
56) and that this hymn must have seen the light of day
much earlier. Moreover, it affirms with undeniable clarity
that the Risen Jesus received "the name above all names"
(v. 9). It is a question here of the unpronounceable name
of God himself,[4] "in order that at the name of Jesus every
knee might bend" (v. 10), a gesture of adoration and of
homage due to God alone.[5]

We could multiply New Testament evidence on this
point. This is not necessary since what is being set forth
here is widely admitted.

b Preexistence of Christ

Let us now turn to the preexistence of Christ (the existence
of Christ before his birth). We find ourselves in an analogous
situation. A Protestant exegete, Martin Hengel, shows that
this doctrine was already well established some fifteen
years after the Resurrection[6]; in order to demonstrate this,
he starts with the hymn in Philippians 2:6-11. Along with the
great majority of exegetes,[7] he thinks that verses 6-7 affirm
the preexistence and the divinity of Christ: "His state was
divine yet he did not cling to his equality with God but
emptied himself to assume the condition of a slave and
became as men are and being as all men are, he made himself humble, yet, even to accepting death, death on a cross."
Hengel comments on this text in the following fashion:

"Paul had undoubtedly founded the community of Philippians in A.D. 49, and it is certain that in the letter addressed six or seven years later to the faithful of this place he had not presented to them a Christ different from the one whom he had preached while founding the community. It follows that this apotheosis of the crucified had already been an accomplished fact during the 40s, and we are tempted to say that in the space of less than 20 years (between the death of Jesus and this "apotheosis"), more activity from a Christological point of view took place than during the entire seven centuries following thereafter in the course of which the dogma of the early Church reached its completion."[8] One could be tempted to contest this interpretation by objecting that a single text, Philippians 2:6-11, is not sufficient to establish it. But this is precisely the point. This text is not an isolated instance.

At least in the opinion of the great majority of exegetes, other texts in the letters of St. Paul affirm the preexistence of Christ. First of all, I Corinthians 8:6, "Still for us there is one God, the Father, from whom all things (come) and for whom we (exist): and there is one Lord, Jesus Christ, through whom all things (come) and through whom we (exist)."[9] This text is not presented as a new teaching about which those for whom it was intended would have been ignorant, as in I Corinthians 15:51: "I will tell you something that has been secret, that we are not all going to die." It is rather the recalling of a doctrine already known. This shows that Paul must have already, from the beginning (around 50-51), preached a preexisting Christ, associated with Creation and, therefore, divine, having been present at the act of Creation in which, by definition, God alone existed.[10]

Finally, the third text in which this doctrine is expressed is 2 Corinthians 8:9: "Remember how generous the Lord Jesus was: He was rich, but he became poor for your sake, to make you rich out of his poverty." The basis of this thought is very similar to the content of Philippians 2:6-11. In speaking of the richness of Christ, Paul could only have had his heavenly preexistence in view since on earth he had always been poor. Let us stress that here also Paul supposes this doctrine as being already known by his readers.

In these three texts, the thought of Paul is particularly
clear. But thanks to these passages, by some type of analogy,
we can recognize this same idea whenever it is being expressed in a more implicit fashion; among others we think
especially of Galatians 4:4; Romans 8:3, and 32.[11]

We can conclude with R. Bultmann: "The doctrine according to which Jesus Christ is the preexisting Son of God
become man . . . is considered by Paul as certain, and the
Philippian Hymn 2:6-11 which is prior to Paul proves that
he is not the first to have introduced it into Christian
thought."[12]

We are purposely limiting ourselves to passages wherein
general agreement obtains among exegetes regarding their
interpretation. These passages sufficiently highlight the
problem. What transpired in less than twenty years that
would give rise to this doctrine about the preexistence and
the divinity of Christ? It is the type of disturbing evidence,
which from the working historian's point of view calls for
an explanation. We have to make the following important
observation on this issue: Even if we accept the opinion of
a small number of exegetes who think that we are not dealing
here with preexistence in texts such as Philippians 2:6-7;
1 Corinthians 8:6; 2 Corinthians 8:9 (cf. notes 7 and 10),
the problem still remains the same. For everyone admits,
without any possible discussion, this clearly evident fact:
In Philippians 2:9-11, indeed, the Risen Christ is adored as
God; the "name above every name" (v. 9) is nothing other
than the ineffable name, Yahweh, and the very genuflection
of heavenly creatures is a sign of adoration reserved exclusively for God (v. 10). The problem is posed then in a
rather pointed fashion. For, as we will see, the early Christian
community was constantly on its guard in its opposition
to the idea of a divinized man.

2 A negative argument: the improbability of the inven-
tion of these doctrines by the community.

a In the pagan environment

At the beginning of this century, exegetes had a ready-
made solution to offer for this problem, namely, the very
rapid appearance of the doctrine according to which Jesus

was a being existing before the creation of the world who had to be placed on the same level as God and adored as he: This doctrine was born and developed not in a Jewish environment, which would have shunned it with horror, but in Greek-speaking Christian communities which came out of the pagan world.

These communities preserved the memory of these "divine men" of paganism, of these mortals who were divinized after their death. Moreover, the doctrine of pre-existence would come into existence in the same environment and its spread would be facilitated by the notion of some type of preexistence of souls, an opinion that was held by a significant segment of pagan philosophical thought.

But, at the present time, this explanation is justifiably being rejected by the great majority of critics. We find reasons for this rejection analyzed, in a very convincing fashion, by the Protestant exegete, Martin Hengel.[13]

Moreover, the chronological argument is by itself alone absolutely decisive. In line with the approach of Martin Hengel, let us recall what has been said previously: The doctrine of Philippians 2:9-11, in which Jesus is adored as God, is presented as a doctrine known by the Philippians. It is certainly the faith that Paul had preached to them when he evangelized the Philippians in the year 49. Since the Hymn is prior to Paul, this proves that this doctrine was widespread among Christian communities by the 50s, which places its origin several years prior to this time. But at this point in history the ideological influence of Christians of pagan backgrounds was nil since, at this particular period, almost all of those overseeing the young Church were of Jewish origin.

b The Jewish milieu

Eliminating the Pagan world, the Jewish world still remains. Among the Jews there are models, texts, *and* doctrines which have served as very effective aids in thinking out and giving expression to the doctrine of the divinity of Jesus and his preexistence. In the Old Testament the Word of God, the Wisdom of God were considered as preexisting and present at the work of Creation: Proverbs 8:22; Wisdom

7:26, Ben Sirach 24:1-5; Isaiah 55:10f; Wisdom 18:15, etc.
All these texts have been understandably utilized by the
New Testament in order to comprehend better the mystery
of Christ, Word, *Verbum*, Wisdom of God. Moreover, the
Judaism, which is contemporary with Jesus, presents an
entire palette of notions concerning the preexistence of
the Messiah, the Law of Moses, the people of Israel, Gehenna,
the Garden of Eden.[14]

But we need to make an absolutely essential distinction.
These notions could have helped a better formulation of
faith in the preexistence and in the divinity of Christ but
they cannot be the *source* of these doctrines. Why? Because,
with respect to the Word, to Wisdom, we are dealing with
attributes personified by a type of literary fiction, as we
can imagine in God a discussion between justice and mercy;
with respect to the Messiah, the Law, Heaven, and Hell,
we are dealing with a preexistence in the plan of God as
Ephesians 1:4, or of a situation analogous to that of the
angels assumed to have existence prior to the creation of
the visible world, and who are only simple creatures, never
equal to God.

But that Jesus might be a divine being having to be adored
like the heavenly Father and not being confused with him,
a Jew would never *on his own initiative*, conceive of anything
as *apparently* contrary to the monotheistic faith of Israel,
this faith which Israel deemed its exclusive privilege and
which it had to manifest to the world. On this point, the
sources make no distinction between the Palestinian Jew
and one from the Diaspora.[15] But to accord a rank and
some divine prerogatives to a man, even after his death, to
declare that he was with the Father before the creation of
the world, all of this was absolutely impossible for a Jew.
This would have been idolatry and there is no parallel
either in the Bible or in the thinking of those rabbis who
were contemporaries of Paul. No man, however great he
might have been, would have been presented as receiving
the name above every name (Yahweh), neither Abraham,
nor Moses, nor any patriarch, nor any prophet. To bend
the knee before him means to adore him, to believe in him,
to convert to him; all of this would have been blasphemous.

Moreover, everything which was suspected of favoring idolatry was rejected with revulsion and the pious Jew had to rend his garments in order to express his horror (cf. Mt 26:65; Acts 14:14; and the indignation of Paul at Athens (Acts 17:16).[16]

It would be tedious and boring, and without any real value, if we were to continue multiplying references. Let us, however, point out those texts of the Bible which express the horror and the righteous indignation on the part of pious Jews when faced with divine honors being accorded to a man: Daniel 3:1-23; Wisdom 14:12-20. Let us recall the specific details on this point which the Jewish historian, Flavius Josephus, (first century of our era) gives us. In order to respect the religious sensibilities of the Jews, Roman armies were ordered not to enter Jerusalem with standards bearing the portrait of the divinized Emperor (*Jewish Antiquities* 18:4, 1; 5, 3; *The Jewish War* 2 9:2). Jews were dispensed from offering worship to the Emperor. And when the Emperor Caligula (37-41 of our era) wanted to impose his worship on Alexandrian Jews and Jews in the Holy Land, he ran up against their desperate resistance which is recounted in detail by the Jewish philosopher, Philo of Alexandria (at the beginning of the first century of our era), as well as by Flavius Josephus (Philo, *Legatio ad Caium* 162:330-67; Josephus, *Jewish Antiquities* 18, 8:1-9; *The Jewish War* 2 10:1-5).

c The Resurrection

If we are to surmount these obstacles, we certainly need a number of extremely strong reasons which will produce crystal clear certitude. Which ones? The Resurrection? As we will indicate, it has unquestionably been an enormous help. But it was not suited to be the foundation of this faith. As unheard of as the fact of the Resurrection might be, it would, without difficulty, find itself compatible with categories of traditional Judaism (cf. 2 Kgs 4:34-36; 13:21). It postulated neither divinization nor preexistence.[17]

In short, for the Jewish milieu, the doctrine of the divinization and of the preexistence of Jesus must have produced exactly the same effect as the great misunderstanding of the inhabitants of Iconium did with respect to Paul and Barnabas ("Gods, in the likeness of men, have descended upon us"). These wanted to honor the two apostles as gods and the apostles, in turn, to show their indignation—"tore their garments" (Acts 14:11-14).

Let us summarize: The rise of this doctrine in the Christian environment of pagan origin is scarcely any longer admitted today; it is impossible for the chronological reasons set forth above (pp. 57-58), since these doctrines are already present when the evangelization of the pagans only began to take place. Its creation in a Christian environment of Jewish origin is ruled out for the reasons which we have just given. However, this doctrine of preexistence and of the divine rank of Jesus really existed less than twenty years after Easter. Does not the historian have the right, even the duty, to say that there remains only one other possible explanation, namely, that it had its origin in a teaching of Jesus himself, so totally incapable of being questioned that it could rise above all the resistance which it would necessarily provoke; and, above all, a teaching confirmed by that event which, to the eyes of the early Christians, constituted the proof that their master had told the truth: the Resurrection of Jesus.[18]

3 A positive argument: indications of an explicit teaching of Jesus to a more restricted circle of disciples regarding his preexistence and his divinity.

By starting with the failure of all the attempts made to explain the very rapid rise of these doctrines except for the appeal to a teaching of the historical Jesus, we have, up until now, attempted to show the probability of such a teaching. Now let us do an inventory of positive indications in favor of a teaching of Jesus having relevance for his divinity and preexistence.

a The existence of a privileged group of disciples within the apostolic college.

It is a well known fact that, among the twelve disciples three did hold a privileged position, Jesus took Peter, James, and John, his brother, with him on three occasions mentioned in the Gospels: the cure of the daughter of Jairus, the Trans-figuration, and the Agony in the Garden of Gethsemane (Mk 5:37; 9:2; 14:33, and parallels); Mk 1:29 additionally observes that these three apostles are witnesses of the miracle of the cure of Peter's mother-in-law; and Mark 13:3 presents them as hearers (with Andrew) of the discourse regarding the end of the world.

It is worth mentioning that we will again find this privileged place in the early Christian community, but with this dif-ference, namely, that James, brother of John, put to death by Herod (around 41), tends to be replaced by the other James, the "brother" of the Lord. Thus Paul calls James, Peter, and John the "columns" of the community (Gal 2:9). Peter and John are involved in the first trial before the Sanhedrin and in the mission to Samaria (Acts 3:1-4; 11 and 8:14-17). This privileged place within the entire group of apostles certainly stems from the closer collaboration that these apostles had previously enjoyed with Jesus.

b Traces of a special teaching reserved to this group

Peter, James, and John are the only witnesses of the Transfiguration and of the Agony. They are, therefore, the only ones to be able to inform the other apostles of it—which gives them a special mission in the transmission of the gospel message. Moreover, to these three witnesses of the Transfiguration Jesus gave the order to "tell no one what they had seen, until the Son of Man had risen from the dead" (Mk 9:9; cf. Mt 17:9). This statement is very sig-nificant for our investigation. Critics are not in agreement regarding the point of knowing whether or not in Mark 9:9 an authentic statement of Jesus is being reported to us. But even if it is a later addition, it translates the conviction that an important aspect of the gospel message had been com-municated, not to all the disciples, but only to three of them, and that its diffusion must be delayed until after the Resurrection.

The discourse on the end of the world, in the Gospel of Mark, is yet another example of an analogous situation. It forms the response of Jesus to a question that the three disciples, Peter, James, and John joined by Andrew (Mk 13:3)

had in a special manner, posed to him. There again whatever may be the differences of exegetes on the historical
nature of this topic, it conveys, at the very least, the opinion
of a certain tradition according to which a restricted group
of disciples would have benefitted from a special teaching
which was not given to all.

We have no teaching of Jesus which, in the Gospels,
would be reserved to a restricted circle of disciples and
which would be concerned with his preexistence and
divinity. But we have seen that the extremely rapid spread
after Pentecost of the doctrine of the preexistence of Jesus
and of his divinity is only historically explainable, in a
plausible fashion, in one way: by virtue of the existence of
a teaching of Jesus on this point. We are tempted to place
this conclusion alongside the fact which has just been
established: the existence of a teaching of Jesus reserved
to a small number of disciples. Why? Because it is in the
very nature of things. Every professor knows that he has, in
his audience, some students who are better endowed than
the rest of the class, and that with them he can "go much
further." And what is true for the teacher in the intellectual
order is also true for the spiritual master.

The twelve, from an intellectual and spiritual point of
view, must have been unequally endowed. If Jesus had to
communicate a teaching which was difficult to understand,
in which misunderstandings and false interpretations
would easily arise—teachings concerning his preexistence
and his divinity—it is normal that he would have chosen
the more highly endowed among his disciples as the first
recipients of this teaching which they would subsequently
be commissioned to spread little by little. Moreover, it is
difficult to see how he would have been able to proceed
otherwise.

And we are equally well aware why the later gospel
tradition had been extremely discreet on the subject of a
teaching of Jesus reserved to a small number of the disciples.
Ancient Jewish writings, contemporaneous or prior to
Christ, which do not form part of Holy Writ, are often of
this type: A great personage from the Old Testament, Moses,
Elias, Baruch, is presented as confiding a secret teaching

to a small band of chosen disciples. He charges this band to transmit this secret to other chosen persons and to publicize it only at an opportune moment. This example is followed in the gospels which are known as *Apocrypha* ("hidden") which claim to present a secret teaching of Jesus, quite superior to that of the official Gospels, and reserved for a public restricted to the initiated. But, from the beginning, Jesus had clearly taken an opposite tack: "I bless you, Father, Lord of heaven and of earth, for having hidden this from the learned and the clever, and revealing these things to mere children" (Mt 11:25). The Gospel is being addressed in a privileged fashion to those most deprived in every area of life. And if, for pedagogical reasons, it had been necessary to pass through a stage of teaching temporarily restricted to a small group, it was important to communicate this teaching as quickly as possible to everyone while their minds would still be open to acceptance. At this time, there no longer existed a reason for preserving the memory of this teaching which was restricted to an elite. Quite the contrary it was most important to forget it lest certain people come to believe themselves commissioned to spread false teaching which would be presented as emanating from the Lord, given to a few and remaining secret up until then. As the history of the primitive Church clearly shows the danger was only all too real.

But, to a certain extent, all of this remains conjecture. We would like to have some more precise indications of a teaching of Jesus relative to his divinity and to preexistence, a teaching communicated to certain disciples and widely diffused, by them, after Easter. The study of the *Johannine tradition* is going to allow us to make headway in this particular regard.

c *The Johannine tradition.*

We have already examined above the testimony of the Fourth Gospel (chap. 1, pp. 9-14). We have tried to show that in this chapter the Johannine Gospel is not similar to the content of the books of Ruth, Esther, Tobias, Judith; the latter present, in effect, an account which had the appearance of history even though, in reality, it is a question of theological doctrine being presented as history in order to render it more capable of being assimilated. The intention of the evangelist, on the other hand, is to communicate to the reader his own conviction: The Jesus that he presents is the real Jesus of Nazareth such as he really was during the course of his earthly life. But we left open the following question: granted that such was the intention of the evangelist, wasn't he, in good faith, deceived by projecting, in an anachronistic manner, upon the Jesus of history what basically constitutes the conviction of his community, namely, faith in the preexistence and in the divinity of Christ? It is now opportune to attempt to respond to this question: John did not deceive himself—even in good faith. The Jesus of history really taught his own preexistence and divinity, perhaps in a clear and explicit fashion, only to "the beloved disciple," while he insinuated it to the others in a more implicit and veiled fashion (cf. the Second Part, chap. 6).

In the reflections which follow and which are intended to support this affirmation, we will be working on the level and from the vantage point of the historian, reserving certain considerations having to do with the intervention of faith for the following chapter.

The historian finds himself before a double fact

1. The very rapid appearance of faith in the preexistence and the divinity of Christ less than twenty years after his death. And this fact does not find a satisfactory explanation in the hypothesis of an invention by the community.
2. The existence of a Gospel, the Fourth Gospel, in which the historian can establish the date or, more exactly, affirm that it had been written, in its present form, by the end of the first century at the latest.[19] This Gospel claims to be the work of an eyewitness of the words and deeds of Jesus; this claim is confirmed by testimonies worthy of faith, extrinsic to the Gospel. And this Gospel affirms that Jesus had clearly taught his preexistence and that he had said: "Before Abraham was, I am." "I and my Father are one."

We have already seen, at great length, the first point.

. The second point deserves a brief treatment.

The Fourth Gospel is presented as the work of a witness, and of a trustworthy witness: "It is this disciple who gives testimony on these things, and it is he who has written them and we know that this testimony is true" (Jn 21:24).

Two remarks on the subject of this text

"This disciple" is referred to in some prior verses as the "disciple whom Jesus loved" (v. 20), the one who at the Last Supper rested on the bosom of Jesus (Jn 13:23f). The tradition, since St. Irenaeus (around 180), identifies this disciple whom Jesus loved, with the apostle John. Further on, we will once again pause to dwell on the extremely important value of the testimony of St. Irenaeus. We merely want to say here that this identification is still accepted today by the great majority of exegetes.[20] This disciple whom Jesus loved is presented in the Gospel as present at the washing of the feet (13:23), on Calvary (19:25-27), during Easter morning (20:2) and at the appearance of Jesus at the lake of Tiberias (21:7). Regarding the piercing of Jesus' side with a lance, he declares "This is the evidence of one who saw it—trustworthy evidence and he knows he speaks the truth—and he gives it so you may believe as well" (19:35). A declaration so explit, so solemn, provides the reader with a choice: Either he believes him, or he considers him an imposter deliberately seeking to mislead.[21]

Here is the testimony of St. Irenaeus on St. John

First of all, he clearly affirms that the author of the Fourth Gospel is indeed John and that John is the beloved disciple who reclined on the bosom of the Lord: "John the disciple of the Lord, the one who rested on his bosom, has himself also published the Gospel during his stay at Ephesus in Asia."[22] But we find here something of greater significance for our purposes. St. Irenaeus had indeed known St. Polycarp, Bishop of Smyrna in Asia Minor, who was a disciple of St. John and had often listened to him. It is important to quote this letter of St. Irenaeus, addressed to a fellow student, Florinus, who had fallen into heresy:

> I saw you in lower Asia with Polycarp, moving in

splendor in the royal court and trying to win favor
with him. I recall the event of that time better than what
has happened recently (for what we learn as children
grows with the soul and becomes one with it), so that I
can tell even the place where the blessed Polycarp sat
and talked, his goings and comings, and manner of his
life, and the appearance of his body, and the discourses
which he gave to the multitude, and how he reported
his living with John and with the rest of the Apostles
who had seen the Lord and how he remembered their
words and what the things were which he heard from
them about the Lord, and about his miracles and about
his teaching, how Polycarp received them from eye-
witnesses of "the life of the *Verbum*" (*tes zoes tou logou*)
and proclaimed them all in harmony with the Scriptures.
These things even then I listened to through the mercy
of God that was granted me, making notes of them
not on paper but in my heart; and ever by the grace of
God I ruminate on them and, I am able to bear witness
before God.[23]

This testimony is extremely valuable. The quality of the
eyewitness of Jesus, affirmed by the author of the Fourth
Gospel, is here confirmed by St. Irenaeus who had heard
those who had listened to John speaking to them of his
relations with Jesus. This testimony can only be placed in
doubt if one has serious reasons for doing so. But *these
reasons* do not exist.[24]

Two remarks

First of all, the testimony of St. Irenaeus is perfectly compatible with the existence of a Johannine school, the existence
of which is more and more accepted by exegetes: some
disciples of the Apostle have set down in writing his teachings and his recollections.

In the second place, as was stressed above (pp. 9-14) he
or the authors of the Fourth Gospel were perfectly capable
of doing what all historians of antiquity did: report the
discourses according to their content and not necessarily
according to their literal terms, and without necessarily re-

porting the exact circumstances in which they had been uttered (time, place, audience). This allows a response to be made to the question that every reader of the Fourth Gospel usually will pose: If Jesus had taught his preexistence and his divinity as openly and as clearly as St. John relates it, why did the other Evangelists have nothing to say about it? We can answer that, very probably, he had done this before a very restricted audience of disciples and in terms better adapted to his disciples' abilities to understand.

Let us conclude and summarize this section which we have called the third stage.

From the strict point of view of the historian, it seems that we can say: The extremely rapid spread of faith in the preexistence and divinity of Jesus, which came about less than twenty years after the death of Jesus, poses a problem from which historians cannot escape. Where does this faith take its origin? The explanation which holds for invention by the community is a dead end. There does remain one possible explanation: We are dealing here with a teaching given by Jesus. This is actually what the Fourth Gospel claims. And the honest historian must say that this claim appears confirmed both by the data of the Gospel itself, and by the witnesses of a tradition worthy of faith (St. Irenaeus).

VIII

Conclusions of the
Historical Inquiry

At the beginning of Chapter V of the Second Part we formulated the following working hypothesis: The Christological affirmations of the New Testament, in particular, those of the Fourth Gospel, regarding the divinity and the preexistence of Christ, correspond to what Jesus thought of himself. And he sought to transmit this conviction by his word and his actions.[1] We have attempted to determine, a priori, how Jesus was obliged to proceed if he wanted to communicate this certitude, given the mentality of his audience, the altogether unheard of character of his message, and the precautions he had to take to avoid false interpretations of a polytheistic type. We have noted that a very gradual method came into play: a very veiled announcement to the crowd, more specific for the disciples already gathered around their Master and who considered him as a prophet transmitting God's Truth. More precise revelation could only be made to a small group of intimates.

We still need to verify this working hypothesis by means of the historical-critical inquiry to which the two preceding chapters have been devoted.

Is this verification conclusive?

About the existence of the first two stages, there is no doubt. The existence of the third stage, however, is less evident: but it was precisely in the course of the inquiry relative to this third stage that an argument was presented which, by itself, is sufficient for establishing the correctness of the exegetical thesis that is being set forth: Jesus was convinced of his preexistence and divinity and he taught it. At the risk of repeating ourselves, let us once again present this argument which seems to be conclusive.

—Faith in the preexistence and in the divinity of the Risen Christ is already present on a grand scale in the Christian community less than twenty years after Easter.

—By this time, the evangelization of the pagan world was at its beginning stages. The influence of Christians of pagan origin in the appearance of this doctrine must be considered as negligible. This evolution therefore took place in the Jewish milieu.

—But the Jewish milieu was essentially allergic to such a doctrine; it, too, greatly resembled the idolatry of divinized men and gods descending upon the earth, a notion which it held in dread and horror.

—Such a doctrine could only take hold as a result of a certitude capable of breaking through all these obstacles: Jesus had taught this doctrine and God had confirmed his teaching by his Resurrection. It doesn't seem possible to present any other solution.

—This is confirmed by the Fourth Gospel. Its author wishes to convince us that the Christ whom he is presenting is indeed the historical Jesus who had the conviction of being the Son of God, God himself, and who had said so. The historian must recognize the solid basis of the arguments which support this opinion (testimonies internal to the Gospel and external attestations: St. Irenaeus).

Having established all of this, the existence of this third stage (the teaching of Jesus to his privileged disciples) becomes so great a probability that we can consider it as established: Only a particularly receptive audience and one already totally devoted to Jesus was capable of receiving this Gospel and, after Pentecost, spreading it in spite of all the obstacles facing it. Moreover, the veiled teaching for the crowd, the more explicit teaching for the disciples which constitute the first and second stage, was intended to sensitize the disciples to a dimension of the person of

Jesus which went totally beyond what the history of the people of God had known in the past. And it is natural that the disciples who were more spiritually in tune with the teaching of Jesus and more attached to him would have wanted to have a more extensive knowledge regarding the content of his enigmatic words. The opposite would have been astonishing and incomprehensible: that no disciple would have shown the least surprise, raised the slightest question regarding the subject matter of these mysterious declarations, and this unaccustomed behavior of Jesus calling God "Abba."

By way of conclusion, are we not able to say: There is an undeniable correspondence between the working hypothesis previously formulated and the consequences which flow from it on the one hand, and the historical inquiry on the other? The probability of this working hypothesis corresponding to reality appears extremely strong, especially in the absence of every other valid explanation of similar data.

IX

The Role of the Holy Spirit

*"I have many other things to tell you,
but you cannot bear them now"* (Jn 16:12).

Up to now, in this Second Part, we are continuing to remain on a purely rational level, accessible to the historian. But this book is being written above all, for believers. The latter, if they fully accept the purely rational level, justifiably refuse to remain there. With regard to the question which is the basis of this book, the believing reader cannot fail to raise the following question: Does this progressive discovery of the divinity of Christ necessarily have, as a possible sole cause, an explicit teaching of Jesus, the product of a perfect understanding of his own mystery? Doesn't this amount to minimizing the role of the Holy Spirit, the interior master? Isn't this tantamount to "down-playing" the importance of certain declarations of Jesus to his disciples, for example: "I have still many things to say to you, but you cannot bear them now, when the Spirit of Truth will come, He will lead you to all truth" (Jn 16:12-13). That the role of the Holy Spirit was essential in deepening the faith of the first Christians in the mystery of the Incarnation is absolutely certain—and we will be more specific on this point later on (infra, p. 74ff). But is the text of John 16:12-13 being applied to the divinity of Jesus, a truth with which the disciples would then be incapable of dealing? This is unlikely. For there would be a contradiction in the Gospel: the divinity of Jesus would be, in one instance, a truth taught by Jesus himself (8:58; 10:30; 17:5) and, at the same time, a doctrine that he would not be able to teach to his disciples

because they would be still incapable of handling it (16:13).[1]
In fact, today the great majority of exegetes explain 16:12-13
by comparing it with the parallel text of 14:26: "I have told
you these things then while I was with you, but the Paraclete,
the Holy Spirit whom the Father will send in my name, will
teach you everything and will recall to you everything that
I have told you"; and 15:15: "Everything that I have learned
from my Father, I have made known to you." Jesus has said
everything that he had to say—but the disciples have not
understood. Jesus would have been able to press the point,
to develop, to detail, to deepen but he did not do this because they were not even capable of assimilating what he
had already told them. He gave the Holy Spirit the mission
of acting interiorly upon the disciples in order that they
might understand, in depth, the words that they had heard
but had not understood. We have, in this case, a familiar
theme of the Fourth Gospel (see 2:22; 12:16; 13:7).

It is exactly in this way that we need to understand the
role of the Holy Spirit in the spread of faith in the divinity
of Christ. The seed had been sown by the teaching of Jesus.
But the soil upon which it had fallen was not yet capable
of receiving it and of allowing it to take root; for that, Easter
and Pentecost were necessary: the Resurrection in order to
open the eyes of the disciples and to make them understand
the greatness of Jesus; Pentecost in order that their intelligence, their minds, and their hearts, illumined and transformed by the Holy Spirit, might finally assimilate a teaching
which had only lightly brushed alongside them without
penetrating their minds and hearts. Let us recur to the
teaching of the Second Vatican Council in its dogmatic
Constitution on *Divine Revelation*:

"Indeed, after the Ascension of the Lord the apostles handed
on to their hearers what he had said and done. This they
did with that clearer understanding which they enjoyed
after they had been instructed by the events of Christ's
risen life and taught by the light of the Spirit of Truth" (*Dei
Verbum* #19). As the conciliar text states, the redaction of
the Gospels had benefitted from this light, even in the
process involved in John's committing the words of Jesus

to writing. We are not dealing with a new doctrine but with a better understanding of Jesus' teaching, one which is more clearly explicit and formulated with more precision, by virtue of the light of the event of Easter and because of the Holy Spirit's activity at Pentecost. As we have already noted (cf. the Introduction) Jesus would have completely recognized the substance of his teaching in the statements of the Fourth Gospel regarding his preexistence and divinity.

Another aspect of the activity of the Holy Spirit must be clearly pointed out. In the formulation of the statements of the New Testament which in a progressively more explicit fashion contain the doctrine regarding the divinity of Christ, it is important to avoid a number of pitfalls—precisely those into which a number of doctrines of the early centuries would ultimately fall and which the Church had to repress: "tritheism," the doctrine reducing the Trinity to a polytheism with three Gods; "Modalism," making of the Father, of the Son, and of the Holy Spirit one divine Person manifesting himself differently in the Scriptures and the history of the People of God. In Scripture, the divinity of Christ is always expressed while maintaining the divine unity of Jewish monotheism and while affirming the distinction existing between the Father and the Son. Later on the Divinity of the Holy Spirit will be recognized under the same conditions. A very special assistance of the Holy Spirit was necessary in order to maintain one's balance on this narrow ledge between two precipices.

X

Who Is the Jesus of History?

METHODOLOGICAL REFLECTIONS

1 Some false evidence

The reader who is somewhat familiar with contemporary exegetical literature will not fail to notice the tremendous differences between the thesis that we are proposing and what he is accustomed to reading, not only in scholarly works intended for exegetes in the field but even in books which are addressed to the nonspecialist public-at-large. At issue here is a fundamental question which touches at the root of the reader's faith: Who was this Jesus of history, the one who lived at Nazareth, preached and taught on the highways and byways of the Holy Land, who suffered under Pontius Pilate, died, and, the reader believes, was raised?

In a recent article, the Dean of the Catholic Theological Faculty of Lyon presents the preoccupations, questions, and the problems of adult catechumens who are seeking baptism.[1] For them, he writes, "the Jesus of history is preferred," and he adds: "On the practical level, their question leads catechesis to make a distinction between the message of Jesus and the Christian message. The latter explains the former and thereby sets forth the importance of the Paschal Resurrection of Christ, his divinity, and the carrying out of his words and deeds."[2] This formulation is altogether correct and it squares with what is contained in the text of *Dei Verbum*, #19.[3] However, one key point needs to be very clearly stressed: There is no difference between the

Christological formulations in the New Testament which are chronologically the latest and what Jesus thought of himself, his person, and his mission. Or more exactly, there is indeed a difference, but it is in the opposite sense: The understanding that Jesus had of himself and of all reality was infinitely richer than that which we find in the New Testament texts, even the most profound and the most fully developed.

The difference regarding which H. Bourgeois, following Vatican II, accurately speaks is not situated on the level of the understanding which Jesus had of himself, as though St. John were explaining what Jesus knew in only a confused fashion. It is situated in between the formulations which Jesus had to adopt, at the beginning, in order to place himself on the very level of his disciples and to make himself understood by them, and the more elaborate statements of Paul and of John. The latter had come to a better grasp of the real depth latent in these imperfect formulations, but their imperfection was necessary by reason of the mentality of an audience which was structured by other ideologies and other expectations.

This precision seems absolutely *essential*. Moreover, it runs totally counter to everything which is currently being written and said in exegesis. In the Third Part of this work we will set forth the nonexegetical reasons for this state of affairs. But here we wish to display a certain number of postulates, rarely explicitly formulated so that their content may clearly appear, and which are only false evidences, really quite debatable. They seem to lie at the origin of the situation being exposed. It becomes a matter of urgency to set them forth clearly and to discuss them. It will then be possible either to abandon or maintain them but doing so totally out in the open.

A first postulate could be called the *principle of the minimum*: Given the fact that there are words of Jesus, the authenticity of which seems certain, and others which are of more-or-less doubtful origin, we possess a more exact portrait of Jesus when we restrict ourselves to the former. This is so typical of false evidence. Is an error by default less serious than an error by excess? Suppose that, in future centuries, the major works of a great modern philosopher are mingled with those of his disciples in such a way that their authenticity is doubtful and that only those are certainly authentic which represent youthful works, without great philosophical interest. Would we have a correct view of the philosophical importance of this thinker by restricting ourselves merely to his certainly authentic works?

In both cases, the only proper attitude consists in attempting to understand to what extent the doubtful texts are rooted in the personality of their author and of seeing if they do not explain an aspect of his thought, already contained in a germinal fashion in the authentic texts.

A second postulate could be called the *privilege of antiquity*: The more a word of Jesus belongs to the earliest strata of gospel tradition, the more chance it has of revealing the authentic teaching of Jesus; and, on the other hand, the more it appears to be later, the more suspect it is.

In this instance also we are dealing with false evidence, one which demands a more carefully nuanced judgment by us. Let us take two extreme cases:

An historic event, such as the Allied landing on June 6, 1944, in Normandy, or a news item such as a railroad disaster. The historian will give greater weight to the accounts of witnesses on the scene and will give less credence to those who only became aware of the event through witnesses of a witness. In this instance, the postulate is really an evidence.

Let us take the case of a thinker, a philosopher of great genius and renown, proposing new ideas, totally foreign to contemporary thought. Suppose that this man had written nothing and he died after a year of teaching. In order to reconstitute his thought we would avail ourselves of two sources: the course notes of his students and the personal works of some disciples, elaborated ten to twenty years later after a long period in which they sought to assimilate the thought of their master. Where would the originality of this genius be best manifested? In the course notes of his students or in the works of his disciples? The answer is clear: the course notes are the work of students whose philosophical universe, structured by prevailing ideas, is

very far removed from the intuition of their professor,
according to the hypothesis being proposed. They would
have taken note especially of what would appear to them
to be in harmony with the universe to which they were
accustomed and would have very poorly reproduced that
which had absolutely no relation to their own mentality—
specifically the new and original aspects of the thought
of the professor. On the other hand, a disciple who had
for twenty years meditated and pondered the insights of
his master, coming to understand them little by little, would
be in a better position to reconstitute at the end of this
long period of maturation, the new and original aspects
of the teaching of the dead master. It is possible, indeed,
that the disciple could add his own ideas to those of the
master. And it is here that the course notes could serve as
a control but, let us insist here, merely a control.

The application to the problem of the Gospel goes without
saying. It is very clear that the "Jesus case" is not connected
to the run-of-the-mill historical fact without any depth, but
to the one which we have just examined.

Moreover, the principle being discussed is valid for the
former case, but not for the latter. It is not any longer valid
for the problem which we are treating, namely, that of the
historical Jesus.

2 The theology of the "divine condescension" (syn-katabasis)

What we have just set forth has already been said in the
past and extremely well said some eighty years ago! Here
is an unfortunately too little known text by Maurice Blondel
which has tremendous relevance for exegetes.

Certainly an honest effort must be made with all
possible circumspection to exhume from the texts the
most direct impressions and the most authentic relics
of the thought and life of Jesus. No doubt I shall be
shown numerous passages in what are called the deepest
strata of the Synoptic Gospels in which Jesus seems
to speak simply as a man of his time; no doubt it will

be maintained that Messianism was the principal vehicle
of his teaching, that the Good Tidings consisted pri-
marily in the proximate advent of the Kingdom, that
the horizon of his preaching seemed to be restricted
as was the outlook of those who received it, to short-
term hopes. But does this mean to say that I must
measure Christ by that first portrait, which after all is
no more than a portrait? For I must remark that Jesus
wrote nothing, so that we have not that direct testimony
of his own thought which a man can leave behind him.
The only way in which we can penetrate into his mind
is through the consciousness of his consciousness on
the part of simple men deeply involved in the prejudices
of their restricted background, and better able, by
reason of their lack of culture, to observe and to maintain the facts, to attach themselves wholeheartedly to a
master and to undergo his personal ascendancy than
to express ideas, to describe an interior life, or to explain
their own faith. . . . Let it not be objected that, if Christ
had been fully conscious of his divinity and possessed
a clear vision of the future, he would have uttered, like
a man of genius who struggles to convey the whole
secret of his soul, more decisive words, echoes of which
would be audible in the Gospels; that would be to forget
that knowledge is not poured ready-made into minds
like words into ears, and that the mystery of God could
not be violated even by revelation itself; it would be a
failure to realize that truth, even though divinely
inspired, cannot commune with human thought except
by becoming incarnate in the contingent forms which
make it, little by little, assimilable; it would be to ignore
this fact that, if the great man's duty is to express his
little human secret, the dignity of God consists in revealing himself to the good will by effortless acts of
power and of immeasurable goodness rather than by
lucid declarations addressed to the intelligence.[4]

The purpose of this paragraph is to sift through all the
implications of this text which is so important for our topic.
And for that the patristic theology of divine condescension

(synkatabasis) offers an adequate structure. This doctrine has been taken over in a very beautiful passage of the Constitution on Divine Revelation (*Dei Verbum*) of the Second Vatican Council.

> "In Sacred Scripture, therefore, while the truth and holiness of God always remain intact, the marvelous "condescension" of eternal wisdom is clearly shown, "that we may learn the gentle kindness of God, which words cannot express, and how far he has gone in adapting his language with thoughtful concern for our weak human nature." For the words of God, expressed in human language, have been made like human discourse, just as the Word of the Eternal Father, when he took to himself the weak flesh of humanity, became like other men."[5]

The fathers of the Church elaborated this theology particularly in order to take account of the connections between the Old and the New Testament. But their great contribution is that of having perceived a permanent law of God's revelation to man.[6] One of the notions which appears most often in their writings is: At each moment of the history of his people, God had been constrained to limit his revelation to what the people were capable of understanding. And even in the very innermost part of this limitation, God had to restrain himself so that the people would be capable of accepting, given mankind's weakness and sin.[7] Through a point of view and a vocabulary which is more up-to-date, we would be able to prolong the thought of the fathers by adding that the revelation of God to man is expressed always by means of *words*, expressions of a *culture*. And this culture has its own proper dynamism, often foreign, even opposed to the proper dynamism of the plan of God. These are the two dynamisms which Jean Guitton, following his master Fr. Pouget, has brought to light and has qualified by calling the former the dynamism of *mentality*, and the latter the dynamism of *spirit*.[8] Each step in God's plan constitutes a sort of symbiosis of both elements. The role of the prophets and other inspired writers is to bring about a progression, little by little, in the mentality while transforming it through the action of the Spirit and by sifting out of it those elements which are inconsistent with Revelation. Thus a new mentality is created, little by little, at the center of which the plan of God will be announced in a more adequate fashion.

This presentation is necessarily schematic. In fact, the development which has just been outlined has not always followed an harmonious growth. There has been some regression, and the passage from one culture to another has most often been the source of serious difficulties.

Be that as it may, the preceding considerations allow us to shed light on the problem of the development of the gospel tradition relative to Jesus' teaching about himself. We see immediately how dangerously erroneous it is to identify the Jesus of history and the Jesus of the historians, intending by the former, the Jesus such as he really was and, by the latter the portrait which can be obtained of him by preferring the earliest testimonies.

Actually between the Jesus of history and the Jesus of the "historians," we can distinguish two degrees of difference:

1. The "condescension" of Jesus, who can reveal about himself only what can be understood and accepted by his audience.

2. The "mentality" of the disciples who read the events, words, and actions on the basis of their conceptions, which are often quite foreign to the reality which they are receiving from Jesus.[9] Deformations, omissions, and coloration due to their mentality flow from this. . . . Only gradually, according to the three stages analyzed above, are the disciples able to come to a better awareness of the personality of Jesus.

Let us now reread the text of Blondel cited earlier. Its importance will be even more apparent, and through it also the profoundly erroneous nature of a particular portrait of Jesus sketched exclusively by strokes the historical-critical authenticity of which can be established—what we have called the Jesus of the historians—in contrast to the real Jesus, the Jesus of history.

In the preceding considerations we situated ourselves on the theological level (the divine "condescension"), and, therefore, on the level of faith.

But we can very easily transpose these considerations into the domain of the historian, who cannot exclude from his/her research the working hypothesis according to which the Jesus of St. John is truly the Jesus of history. This is precisely the working hypothesis at the beginning of this Part (above p. 33) and which has been consistently justified from the point of view of the historical method. Moreover, the considerations proposed will be able to help the believer to understand that from the point of view of true historical science, it is legitimate to challenge the Jesus of the "historians" in order to recognize the real Jesus of history, the Jesus of the Fourth Gospel. We will not allow ourselves to be affected by the apparent opposition which exists between the Jesus of the earliest traditions and that of the Fourth Gospel: The elements set forth in the course of this chapter permit not only an explanation of this, but allow his normal and inescapable character to be taken into account.

We are finally able to conclude: There is identity between the Jesus of history and the Jesus of the Fourth Gospel who believed that he was God and who taught it. Christian tradition is unanimous in affirming it. The serious historian can, first of all, show that this statement of tradition is not contradicted by honest historical research. But he can go further and state that this affirmation corresponds to historical reality.

THE THIRD PART
Faith of the Church and the Modern Mentality

XI

Jesus Is Truly Man

What does to be truly man signify?

In this Third Part we would like to take up a certain number of difficulties no longer in the exegetical realm but, to use the vocabulary of modern theology, in the hermeneutical realm. Under this somewhat complicated word there lies hidden a very simple reality: How actualize, make current this affirmation of the Church's unanimous tradition, which is also confirmed by a solidly rational exegesis: not only is Jesus God, but he knows it and he taught it. It has often been correctly stated: It is not enough to repeat the formulas of our Creed, the definitions of the great councils. It is important that they mean something for us, that these formulas have a content which nourishes our faith and enlightens our life, our Christian behavior. But then we find ourselves up against a very great difficulty, stemming from our precomprehension.[1] We can state it, in this fashion: Jesus is truly man; he totally shared our human condition with the exception of sin (cf. Heb 4:15). But if Jesus had an awareness of being truly God, equal to the Father, pre-existing in glory from all eternity, then he no longer is truly man, he no longer is the one who is in every way except sin made to resemble his brothers.

This difficulty can be stated in a less dogmatic and more biblical fashion: If Jesus of Nazareth, during his earthly life, had truly been the one whom the Fourth Gospel portrays, then he feigned sharing our human condition; he really didn't assume it.[2]

In reality who is he?

1 The role of precomprehension

Into the affirmation of our faith, Jesus is truly man, we necessarily introduce our own notion of man.

But this notion of man depends on our mentality, on our culture, on the great ideological currents which pervade the intellectual atmosphere in which we live. It varies according to time and according to place. Often it is questionable. One of the purposes of the Word of God in Scripture is precisely to challenge us and to call into question *in all areas* the precomprehension stemming from an environment, from a culture, from a mentality often formed by currents, the guiding force of which is alien to the Christian gospel and opposed to it. And this is particularly true for our own conception of man. If Jesus is truly man, it is he who taught us who man is; it is not we who determine a priori, with the aid of our precomprehension, criteria which Jesus had to meet in order to be truly man.

2 A text of Hans Urs von Balthasar

At the beginning we stated that as far as possible with some exceptions we will avoid polemics. Here is one. The situation is much more difficult because we are dealing with a very great Catholic theologian, Hans Urs von Balthasar. We totally subscribe to these lines of Cardinal de Lubac: "When, at long last, the current fever will have come down . . . and so many sensational writings will be seen as nothing, the writings of Fr. Urs von Balthasar will attest that the middle of the twentieth century, for all its miseries, was a great period for Christian reflection.[3]

The following is what this great theologian wrote in a text which has been very frequently cited by a good number of exegetes and dogmaticians: "Jesus is a real man and the inalienable nobility of man is to be able and to want to project freely the plan of his existence into a future about which he is ignorant. If this man is a believer, the future into which he throws himself and projects himself, is God in his liberty and his immensity. To deprive Jesus of this chance and to have him advance towards an end known in advance, and distant only in time, would end up by depriving him of his dignity as a man."[4]

Is this true? Does it really "deprive man of his dignity" to have him advance toward an end known in advance and distant only in time"? If the answer is affirmative, then all the fathers of the Church, all the saints, all the theologians of antiquity, of the Middle Ages and of modern times up to the middle of the nineteenth century, all have deprived Jesus of his dignity as man. Not only Catholics, but theologians and teachers in Protestantism and Orthodoxy. For the affirmation of St. John was clear and precise for them. "Jesus, knowing everything that was going to happen to him . . ." (Jn 18:4). None of them had the least doubt; this little clause said exactly what it meant: the man Jesus, the son of Mary, knew everything that was going to happen to him. And we can say exactly the same thing about predictions concerning the Passion, with its specific content: the mocking, the spitting, the scourging (Mk 10:34 and parallels). *All* have read in these texts the clear affirmation that Jesus knew in advance, in detail, what was soon going to transpire: the passion with all its various episodes, being handed over to Roman authorities, the Crucifixion and the Resurrection.

We come now to the question: Is it really necessary to admit that all of those who believed that Jesus went forward "towards an end known in advance and only distant in time," did not know what "a real man" in his "nobility" and in his "dignity was"—St. Irenaeus, St. John Chrysostom, St. Augustine, St. Leo the Great, St. Bernard, St. Thomas, St. Bonaventure, as well as Luther, Calvin, and Melanchthon?

Did we really have to wait until the twentieth century in order to discover what Jesus needed to be and to do in order to be a real man in all his nobility and his dignity?

In this regard would we pretend to be superior to the evangelists themselves, and not only to John but also to Mark, Matthew, and Luke, who believed and taught naively that Jesus had predicted the denial of Peter, the treason of Judas, the mocking, the scourging, the spitting, his death on a cross and his Resurrection?

3 The objection based upon texts concerning the lack of knowledge of Christ

I realize that someone is going to respond: You favor certain texts and you forget others: What are you going to do about the ignorance of the day of judgment, about the agony in the garden, about the cry from the cross: "Why have you abandoned me"?—I'm not forgetting these texts, they will be treated further on and in detail (chap. 14, p. 118ff). For the moment, let us just say that the fathers and their successors also knew these texts and the problems that they posed. As we have seen above, they were no less unanimous in their conviction. The objection that we just mentioned was known to them. It was raised in the second century by the pagan Celsus whose arguments they read in the treatise written by Origen to refute him. Concerning the agony in the garden, Celsus wrote "It is clear that nothing could have been difficult or painful for Him since He was God and willed it all. Why does He seek to avoid death which He dreaded by saying: 'Father if it is possible, let this chalice pass from Me.' "[5] Thus we can see, in all of its clarity, and in a total understanding of the situation, how the fathers, the theologians of the Middle Ages and of modern times were fully aware of all these difficulties when they held firmly the positions which we have just recalled. And the solutions which they employed to reconcile both aspects of the behavior of Jesus seem destined to be preserved, due provision being made for some nuances.

4 Precomprehension and "the progress of modern exegesis"

Another objection which will certainly be made permits us to go even farther, to the very core of this problem: It is not, some will say, a precomprehension of the man which causes us to abandon the conviction of the Fathers and of the great theologians of the past, rather it is the advances made by modern exegesis.

These advances no longer allow us to hold, as historical, the presentation of the evangelists, not only the portrait of Jesus in John, but numerous details in the three evangelists: in particular, the image of Jesus knowing, in detail, all the episodes involved with his Passion.

This does not seem to be correct. We have attempted to show this in the Second Part of the book concerning the conviction that Jesus had of being God; and we have been able to see that the opinion on this subject of unanimity in Christian tradition can invoke in its favor more solid exegetical and historical-critical arguments, it seems, than the opposite opinion. We could make the same case for other currently debated issues: Jesus' knowledge of the future, secrets of hearts, the conviction that he was to die for the salvation of all mankind, his desire to establish the Church, etc. The case would be appreciably the same and the results quite similar.

It is precisely here that the precomprehension of the exegete comes into play. As we have already emphasized (above, chap. 1, p. 11ff and note 3, chap. 1), the reading of the biblical text by the exegete is always colored and conditioned by his own precomprehension which stems from his environment, from his culture, and from his previously firm convictions. This precomprehension plays no role when exegetical research arrives at results which are absolutely certain and indisputable, as in the mathematical sciences, for example. But this case is the exception. Generally, we only reach more-or-less probable results. Very often there is disagreement between exegetes of the same competence, seriousness, and good faith, even when they use the same methods and communicate their studies to one another. This can only signify one thing, doubt. And thus the fatal mistake of the exegete is to opt for the solution conforming to his own particular precomprehension of the problem. It is also significant that, with respect to the biblical texts, the interpretation of which is based on denominational divisions, the exegete always ends up with the interpretation of his own church, and with serious scientific reasons to boot: The exceptions to this can be counted.

That is why the method followed here (above p. 1) seemed preferable: To start with the tradition of the Church and show, from the exegetical point of view, its solid basis. This also explains the attitude of the majority of exegetes *vis-à-vis* the problem which concerns us: By starting with a particular precomprehension of man, they end up with an exegetical solution which verifies this precomprehension with respect to the man Jesus. That is why, to the question: What does it mean for Jesus, "to be truly man," we respond not by examining the precomprehension stemming from our modern-day mentality, but by examining more than twenty centuries of Christian tradition in order to determine what is constant and unchanging about it.

5 What does "Jesus is truly man" signify for Christian tradition?

We can cover this point very quickly; certain aspects are sufficiently evident so that it is merely necessary to enumerate them; others, more directly connected with our subject, have already been treated in detail (*see* the First Part).

(a) Jesus shared the lot of every man in the area of joys as well as physical and moral sufferings which are the lot of all humanity, including and above all, death.

(b) Jesus had been infinitely superior to all men in all aspects of the moral life; in the intimacy of his relation with the Father; in his holiness.

(c) Since in every way he is truly man, Jesus is distinguished from other men by certain aspects of his life and activity: the Virgin birth, the power to perform miracles, etc.

(d) In the area of knowledge we can generally distinguish two periods in the tradition of the Church.

(1) In an early period, basically before the Council of Chalcedon, we distinguish the knowledge that Jesus of Nazareth had *as God*, a knowledge infinitely perfect and complete, equal to that of the Father, and that which he had *as man*, in which he can exhibit ignorance and uncertainties.

(2) In a second period (especially after Chalcedon, but even before, among some fathers) we more and more discover the insufficiency of the preceding outline in spite of its accuracy. Since Jesus of Nazareth had at his disposal a knowledge which he possessed as God, this implies that this divine knowledge is expressed by human words, human

concepts, products of a human intelligence; and this supposes that the divine understanding of the Word is communicated to the human understanding of Christ according
to its limited capacity. This becomes altogether evident
after the definitions of the Council of Chalcedon which
affirm the coexistence of two natures in Christ, at the same
time God and man, without confusion, each preserving
its own properties. From then on the classic formula which
we find again in St. Leo[6]: "Jesus said that as God" must be
improved upon and made more precise: "Jesus said that as
a Man who knew that he is God." From then on, the entire
Christian tradition, in one way or another, will adopt the
content of the formulations of St. Fulgentius (above, p. 18).
Jesus as man knew everything that God knew, but according
to the limited manner in which the knowledge of all human
intelligence is exercised, however perfect it may be.

(e) It will be objected that even if it is a matter of a constant in Christian tradition, we are very far from Hebrews
4:15. We can answer: Is this all that certain? Let us make
two remarks on this question.

(1) Hebrews 4:15 speaks above all of the sufferings, of
the trials, that Jesus shared with other men; and this is not
attained by what has just been said.

(2) This remark places us on the road which leads to
the guiding principle which, from the time of the Synoptic
Gospels, unifies the whole Christian tradition regarding
the point which we are studying: How and to what extent
did Jesus share in our present human condition? An answer
can be formulated with the assistance of the Pauline theme
of the new Adam (cf. 1 Cor 15:45-49; Rom 5:12-21): to be
like us was not, for Jesus, an end in itself; this similarity
was ordained for one purpose, to assume the headship of
sinful humanity in order to lead it to the Father by making
it share in his loving obedience and his holiness (cf. Rom
5:19). Moreover, Jesus was like us in everything, *save* in
what was necessary according to God's plan to accomplish
his mission as Savior. And this last point, already in the
Synoptics, implies not only perfect holiness, but even the
full and total knowledge of the plan of God, of his own
mystery and what Jesus had received from the Father in

order to manifest, in a better manner, who he was: the virgin birth, the gift of being able to perform miracles, cures, knowing the innermost thoughts of human hearts, etc.

We still have to treat what, in the eyes of many, constitutes the most serious objection against the doctrine according to which Jesus had full knowledge of his divinity and of the unfolding of history. It can be formulated in this manner: The sufferings, the agony, the anguish, the death of Christ are perhaps real—materially, physically, biologically in some way. But they become insignificant. We frequently hear and see mention of that stupid enough story about a boy, who when asked in catechism class to express what Jesus thought of on the cross, answered "What did He think? 'I don't give a damn about it; in three days I will rise.' " In the mouth of a child ten years old this response causes one to smile. But it doesn't deserve to be quoted in serious publications by way of support for the objection formulated above, one which we are going to examine.

XII

The Knowledge and Suffering of Jesus

We are going to present and prove the following position: The knowledge that Jesus had of his divinity, of his Resurrection, and of his future coming in glory did not make his sufferings less severe, or even unimportant, as the statement of the child in catechism class just cited might lead one to believe and as is frequently pointed out by exegetes and theologians. *It is the opposite which is true.* The Passion of Jesus becomes trifling and trivial if we contest or minimize the knowledge that Jesus had of his own mystery, of his eminent dignity as Son of God, of his mission as universal Savior and new Adam, head and chief of the new humanity.

Actually when reduced to sufferings of an ordinary man who is convinced of being the legate of God and who wishes to be faithful even unto death to what he believes to be his mission, these sufferings and the death of Jesus do become something extremely commonplace: so many men have suffered much more than he. Jesus had only been in agony for a few hours on the cross, while those who were crucified, during his lifetime, suffered several days; and it was absolutely forbidden to shorten their sufferings by giving them the *coup de grace* for which they continuously pleaded. How many deaths have been more atrocious than his own, preceded by longer sufferings, sufferings which were more intense and accompanied by moral sufferings more trying still like that of the condemned man in whose presence over a protracted period of time, his wife, his children, and his parents are going to be martyred? It's useless to persist on this point.[1]

1 The constant teaching of the Church

We can, it seems, affirm that there is a constant in the teaching of the Church, not only in her theological and doctrinal tradition but also and especially in her spiritual tradition; the life, the testimony, and the writing of the saints; and in the liturgical life of the Church. We can express it in this fashion: Whatever may be the intensity of the suffering of a person, Jesus marches always before him/her as the example to follow, the model to imitate. This conviction appears already in texts such as Hebrews 12:3-4 and 1 Peter 2:21. St. Thomas Aquinas gathers together and summarizes the whole Christian tradition when he poses this question, to which he responds affirmatively; did the suffering of the Passion of Christ surpass all other sufferings?[2] Why? A detail in the accounts of the Passion can place us on the right path in order to give a proper response: We read in Mark 15:23: "(. . .) and they gave him wine mixed with myrrh, but he did not take of it." This precision, the historicity of which is not contested by anyone, corresponds to a very clearly attested custom of the period; and commentators usually cite the principal texts which mention it. In Israel, a drink which acted as an anesthetic, in order to alleviate his sufferings, was frequently given to the condemned man. Jesus refused it.[3] Why? A man who is going to undergo a painful operation and who refuses a tranquilizer, an anesthetic, will very easily be accused of masochism. Is this the case with Jesus? Certainly not. But then it is important to admit that Jesus not only undergoes his sufferings, but he accepts them willingly because in his eyes, they have, in God's plan, a meaning, a role, an end. And it is for this reason that he does not wish that they be in any way reduced. Even during his ministry Jesus had clearly said that he was impatient in anticipation of these sufferings, this death. He would even go so far as to say: "It is a baptism that I must receive and great my distress[4] is until it is over"[5] (Lk 12:50).

In no way is this masochism; there is no morbid attraction

to suffering. Suffering is in itself an evil which, by necessity, is to be avoided and fought against. But it can be the cause of tremendous good when it is the expression of love: "There is no greater love than to give one's life for those whom one loves" (Jn 15:13). This magnificent good is the salvation, the redemption of mankind. It is this which Jesus would affirm several times: "The Son of God did not come to be served, but to serve and to give his life in ransom for a multitude" (Mk 10:45; Mt 20:28); "This is my blood, the blood of the covenant, which is going to be poured out for the multitude for the remission of sins" (Mt 26:28; cf. Mk 14:24).[6]

We see, then, that we cannot *reduce* the Passion and the death of Jesus, *such as he experienced them himself*, to their purely historical dimension, as events such as they appear to witnesses, to spectators: the death of a prophet claiming to have been sent by God and even to being the Son of God, a friend of publicans and of sinners, condemned unjustly to sufferings and to an ignominious death, and who accepted this death rather than betray his mission. This dimension certainly is real; it is important, and we have no right to minimize it. But it does not reach the true depth of the mystery. If only this dimension existed, it is true that the perspective of a resurrection in a few hours would do away with the awesome nature of Jesus' suffering, all the more so since on the simple biological level, many people in the world have suffered much more before dying than he did.

2 Jesus always goes before us

But the situation changes if we admit what we have demonstrated above: Jesus truly possesses awareness of being the one who is presented to us in the Fourth Gospel: God, Son of God, who came to save the world. And in this work of salvation, the sufferings of Jesus achieve their complete dimension. We are dealing with the passion of a divine person suffering in the human nature which he had assumed on our behalf.

Jesus is in total solidarity with our sinful humanity by assuming not sin but suffering and death, the consequences of sin, in order to make us participants in his life as Son of

God. This implies that Jesus suffers as head of his body, as
shepherd of his flock, in such a way that whatever may be
the intensity of his suffering, man finds, in Jesus, the one
who has gone before him on this road. This is the way that
Paul understands the suffering of Christ:

> For him, I have accepted the loss of everything, and I
> look on everything as so much rubbish if only I can
> have Christ and be given a place in him. I am no longer
> trying for perfection by my own efforts, the perfection
> that comes from the law but I want only the perfection
> that comes through faith in Christ, and is from God
> and based on faith. All I want is to know Christ and
> the power of his resurrection to share his sufferings
> by reproducing the pattern of his death" (Phil 3:8-11).

It is this infinite dignity of the one who suffers which gives
to his sufferings their unique and unsurpassable intensity:
the physical sufferings of the Passion, the sorrowful character
of which comes not only from his wounded body but also
and above all from his heart tortured by the fact that men
have rejected his love; the sorrow caused by the sin of the
world, for Jesus sees infinitely better than all of us both
the hatred of God that it contains and the ravages that it
produces in the hearts of men and the evils that it causes
in the world.

Finally and, above all, Jesus experienced supreme sorrow
when he cried out: "My God, my God, why have You for-
saken me"? Not that Jesus had ever been abandoned by
the Father and had lost certitude of being his beloved Son,
but he wanted to share the suffering of those who live this
total abandonment in order that they might be able to find
a model in him. For this, he had agreed that the light of
the presence of his Father burn only in the innermost, the
most inaccessible abyss of his Being without shining upon
his intelligence, his will, his sensibilities plunged, as they
were, in the most impenetrable darkness. Consequently,
many of the saints have been invited by Jesus to share in
this suffering; their testimony is a light for us which allows
us to understand a little better this tremendously mysterious

aspect of the Passion of our God.

We still need to raise one final question. *How am I, myself, in my life affected by the Passion and the death of Jesus?* Is Jesus simply a noble example for me to imitate in his struggle against injustice, oppression, in his activity in behalf of the poor, the marginalized, those beyond the law? Is this an invitation to enter into this way, like him, to the point of sacrificing life? That this particular aspect exists cannot be contested. But are we thereby able to justify the *unique* character of the Passion of Christ for Christians?

One evening I attended a conference given by a renowned Marxist who drew a comparison between Jesus and Spartacus, a gladiator who had fomented a slave revolt, which 100 years before Jesus Christ caused the entire Roman Empire to tremble. He was finally apprehended and killed. And the speaker demanded: "which of the two had been more active, more ardent in his struggle in favor of the poor and of the oppressed? Jesus or Spartacus"? We are only able to set this question aside by placing it on an altogether different level, the level on which the apostle St. Thomas places it when he confesses: "My Lord, and my God" (Jn 20:28). It is because he knows that he is God that Jesus can reveal to me and show me through his Passion and death the infinite tenderness of the heart of God. When the mystery of evil, of sin, of innocent suffering weighs me down and deeply disturbs me, I can contemplate God crucified. He doesn't give me a philosophical solution to a mystery which remains impenetrable but a response which is life, commitment, love, total surrender. Evil is no longer pure non-sense; it spills over into life; it is a passage toward life. Jesus, God-with-us, Emmanuel, wanted to share our miserable condition and has given sense to it, according to the twofold dimension of the French word *sens*: signification, direction. And he is not only with me, he is in me: "With Christ I am nailed to the cross; I live now not I but Christ lives in me" (Gal 2:20). Jesus, my God, asks me to allow him to live and act in me, in order to unite my suffering to his own, my death to his own, in an offering of love to the Father for the salvation of my brothers. Jesus, living in me, incites in my heart the desire to suffer with him, like him, in the same way that he inspired this desire in the heart of Paul (Phil 3:10), because he wishes that I rise with him in real life, already begun on this earth before it fully blossoms forth in heaven, and because he wishes that in him I may be the source of life for all my brothers.

XIII

What Does "Did Jesus Know that He Was God" Really Signify?

1 The problem

"Before Abraham was, I am"; "Father, give me the glory which I had with you before the world began." It is not without reason that we hesitate to use these two statements of Jesus, quoted in the Fourth Gospel (Jn 8:58; 17:5), as declarations corresponding to what Jesus thought about himself, declarations that he had made or that he could have made. Why: Because we can give a dogmatic and therefore abstract content to the formula of the Council of Chalcedon: one single person, at the same time true God and true man; but it seems very difficult for us to give an existential, concrete, psychological reality to these dogmatic concepts. This appears to be one of the reasons why so many of our contemporaries, theologians or exegetes, as well as many nonspecialists, clergy or lay, more or less openly reject a formula such as: Jesus knew that he was God.

Let us try to specify this even further by entering more deeply into the reasons for this more-or-less explicit refusal.

In order to do so let us mention the discussion which one day pitted me against an atheist who knew his theology very well (at one time he had taught it). He wished to prove the absurdity of the dogma of the Incarnation especially as it had been formulated by the Council of Chalcedon. He started with an article of St. Thomas Aquinas in the *Summa Theologica* (III, quest. 3, art. 7) in which the latter poses the following question: "Can a single divine person

assume two human natures"? He responds affirmatively
since "nothing is impossible with God." In a previous
writing,[1] St. Thomas had raised the same question: "Would
it have been possible for God to have become Incarnate
in Jesus and in Peter"? The response is equally affirmative,
for the same reason. But finally he was asked: "Would Jesus
and Peter then be two men or only one"? The response
was differently formulated in both writings although it was
identical in its content. In the earlier writing, there would
have been, in this case, two men forming one single person.
According to the *Summa*, there would only be one man
existing in two different human natures.[2] My questioner
pursued: "We should be thankful to St. Thomas Aquinas
for having examined, with total logic, all the possibilities
involved in the dogma of the Incarnation. The demonstra-
tion is clear as far as I'm concerned: the absurdity of the
result proves the absurdity of the point of departure. This
dogma is absurd."

Finally, there was a long silence. I was completely bowled
over by this problem which I had never envisaged and I
didn't know how to respond. A young girl who was sitting
in the audience responded in my stead: "Is it all that absurd?
Two human beings who would no longer be anything except
one in God? Isn't this the deep wish of all love—that those
who love each other are no longer anything other than
one? Isn't this the perfect realization of what we try to live
out through love of God and brotherly love; the second
commandment is like onto the first, and you shall love your
neighbor as yourself"?

The discussion was interrupted by the arrival of a friend.
But this intervention on the part of the young girl demonstrated something essential: Beyond the apparently strange
and unreal hypothesis proposed by my questioner, it in-
dicated a way to understand the mystery of the psychological
"me" of Jesus of Nazareth: the mystique of love.

2 The mystical life and the consciousness of Jesus

It is trite to state that there are various common points
in the religious experience of mystics belonging to different
religions, to various times and places, without there being

any possibility of showing the slightest direct or indirect contact between them.

But one very astonishing area in common merits particular attention since it can shed light on the subject which we are considering. It is a tendency common to certain mystics, whether Moslem or Christian: a tendency to identify oneself totally with God. The mystic declares: I, myself, am God. As has very well been shown by those who have studied these mystics and examined in context the formulas which have a particularly pantheistic flavor to them, we are not dealing with a declaration of the philosophical order but with an adequate formulation of an impulse of love. Love unites the mystic so powerfully to God that there is almost total unity, not in the order of existence, but in the order of action: love, will. We find such formulations in Islam. It is enough merely to refer my readers to the beautiful book which G. C. Anawati and L. Gardet devote to Islamic mysticism.[3] These authors studied, among others, the presentation of one Bistami (who died in 874),[4] those of the celebrated martyr Al-Hallaj[5] (858-922) and that of Ibn al-Farid (1181-1235).[6]

In Christian mysticism, one of the most celebrated names is that of the Dominican Master Eckhart (1260-1328).[7] There can be no possibility here of analyzing such a complex system of thought about which specialists are far from being in agreement about every detail. What is certain is that the judges who condemned him reproached him for formulas in which the just man is identified with God, creating, with him, the heavens and the earth, begetting the eternal *Verbum*.[8] Whatever may be the proper correctness of such a reproach, it is certain that we can find in his sermons a number of almost identical formulas: "I was cause of myself and of all things"; "God and I are one."[9] But, given the context, it is nonetheless certain that it is a question here *not* of speculative theology but of the mystical experience of union of love with God; a union which appears so strong, so profound, so intimate, that the language of identity appears the least inadequate of all possible languages, even if we recognize how false it is from the point of view of the religious doctrine and deeper reality; and Master Eckhart,

professor of theology, Master of the Sorbonne, disciple of
St. Thomas and St. Albert the Great, knew this better than
anyone.

We are restricting ourselves to a quick overview of a few
people who are rather well known. But there are other
examples which could be presented, examples of people
from various other spiritual streams.

There is certainly something authentic in these "way-
out" formulas, about which even the authors themselves
realize the presence of exaggeration: the experience of a
union with God, of a unity with God so profound, so power-
ful, that proper theological formulas are not capable of
expressing it adequately. We also find some very strong,
theologically unassailable formulas in a celebrated treatise,
almost as well known as the *Imitation of Jesus Christ*, the
De Adhaerendo Deo (about intimate union with God), for a
long while attributed to St. Albert the Great (died in 1280),
but which is undoubtedly later: "The love of God has the
value of uniting and of transforming. It transforms the one
who loves into the one who is loved and the one who is
loved into the one who loves. One becomes the other
inasmuch as it is possible to do so."[10]

What follows are the consequences which one can draw
from this short incursion into the area of mysticism:

1. Mystics such as Hallaj and Eckhart could give an
existential and real content to the formula: "I am God" as
the least inadequate expression of their experience of union
with God through love, even though they were well aware
that they were not God.

All the more reason, for someone, who we believe is
truly God to be able to give a real existential content to
this formula, as really expressing what he is and what he
experiences; and this, in an infinitely deeper more inexpressible fashion than the most perfect mystics.

2. The mystical knowledge through the union of love
with God is a less imperfect human analogy allowing us to
gain some type of glimpse of the knowledge which Jesus
had about his divinity.

Let us develop this second point a little further in order

to understand better the thrust and the limits of the analogy offered by mystical knowledge.

For the genuine mystic, there is an identification which becomes *more and more strong in the area of the will*, between the will of man and the will of God. In this area there is no barrier, there is no limit. The mystic has the conviction—which is fundamentally correct—that he can constantly make progress, by the grace of God, to the point of total identification.

In the realm of intelligence, there is likewise progress but in a very different way: It is a question of a knowledge which progresses by means of stripping, by the abandonment of every image, of every representation, of every idea; of a knowledge in which man more and more feels the impassable distance which separates the creature from the creator, from zero to infinity. But at the same time, paradoxically, this knowledge becomes more and more aware of the fact that God is really present, living, acting, loving, in the very intimate recesses of his creature: I'm not God, but I am in God and God is in me.

We can, thus, catch a glimpse of how the psychology of the mystics allows us to better understand that psychology of Jesus; and it can actually give us a certain, albeit very feeble, notion of the knowledge that he had of his divinity. Let us note, first of all, that this comparison is not new—it is even classic—and many theologians make use of it or at least mention it.[11] Fr. Garrigou-Lagrange spoke of the "superior impersonality of the saints," a formula that he explained in this way: "the full development of the human personality consists in losing oneself in that of God," and he shows how this law of holiness allows us to understand better the divine personality of Jesus.[12] The philosopher, Henri Bergson, in *Les Deux Sources de la morale et de la religion*, defines the mystic as "a soul at the same time acting and being acted upon whose liberty coincides with divine activity."[13] We see, moreover, that what Christian faith affirms about Christ constitutes, as it were, a plentitude, an absolute perfection with respect to what the saints, who felt themselves more and more called to lose themselves in God, to be melted like wax into him, actually experienced.

The human personality of Jesus is totally assumed by the divine personality of the Son of God, and Jesus can say in all truth, what Hallaj and Eckhart expressed in formulas which are theologically false, but which, in their eyes, were those which were the least imperfect for expressing what they were living out. But we need to insist upon the fact that in the case of the mystics as in the case of all the saints that we are dealing with an experience of the love of God. It is through the logic of love, at the heart of the very source of love, that we can better understand the knowledge that Jesus had about his divinity: as the supreme plenitude about which the experience of the love of the saints only furnishes a pale comparison.

3 Filial love and self-awareness in Jesus

If we return to the gospel, and if we once again take up the texts in which we have seen that Jesus manifested his divinity by adapting himself to the capacity of his audience, there is one thing which is quite striking. Jesus doesn't speak of himself, his own greatness, his own dignity, but only of his relationship with the Father. We merely have to look once again at the texts which were studied in the Second Part in order to be convinced of this. The same is true in St. John: "Father, come and glorify me with the glory that I had with you before the creation of the world"; "My Father and I are one" (Jn 17:5; 10:30).

Jesus does not manifest himself directly as God, but as Son of God, Son of the Eternal Father, equal to the Father. It is in this fashion, by manifesting his bond of filial love for the Father that he reveals his divinity. This is absolutely essential. Jesus doesn't have an awareness of being God by some sort of reflex consciousness, but through his glance and look of filial love toward his Father. This point needs to be strongly emphasized. According to traditional doctrine, in the mystery of the Holy Trinity, the three divine persons have in common only their *relationships* to the other persons.[14] The Son has in common only his relationship of love to the Father. And if we affirm, with Christian faith, that the person of Jesus of Nazareth is in identity the Second Person of the Blessed Trinity, this means that the person of Jesus of Nazareth is defined solely by his filial relations of love to the Father. There is then a fundamental difference between Jesus and us. For man, for us, the person is the center of autonomy; for Jesus, it is dependence. It is the filial relation of love to the Father which constitutes Jesus of Nazareth as a divine person, that is to say as God.

This is essentially the consciousness that Jesus of Nazareth has of his divinity, in his psychological and existential dimension: we can say that it is radically impossible for Jesus himself to glance upon himself.[15] Since he is a divine person who is only the relationship of love to the Father, he is himself, Jesus of Nazareth, related to the Father by all the fibers of his being, totally and integrally. And certainly Jesus himself is aware of himself; he had an awareness of himself, infinitely greater and better than we. But it is an awareness which is uniquely and totally filial. He is aware of himself in and through the Father, without any backward glance upon himself. It is in his look of love toward the Father that Jesus himself is aware of himself, totally, since he only exists by the Father, in the Father, for the Father. Jesus knows that he is God: this formula, however correct it is, is nevertheless, inadequate. It would be better to say: In his look of love toward the Father Jesus sees that the Father has given everything to him, everything that he is, everything that he possesses and that this total gift is completely reciprocal[16]: "All I have is yours and all you have is mine" (Jn 17:10).

Understood in this way, the awareness that Jesus possesses of his divinity is not some sort of psychological monstrosity which definitively distanced the Man-Jesus from our earthly condition. It is on the contrary the dazzling summit of the total gift of himself to God through love, which is the vocation of every human creature.

And the reciprocal total gift, which is the desire of all love, is realized fully in the total gift of the Father to the Son and of the Son to the Father, a gift that Jesus of Nazareth, the Son in his human nature, receives totally and offers totally.[17]

XIV

Knowledge and Ignorance of Jesus

1 Preliminary remarks

For many exegetes and modern theologians, it is necessary to choose between two faces of Jesus. One which declared at Gethsemane: "Father, if it is possible, let this cup pass from me" (Mt 26:39), thereby seeming not to know both the will of the Father and what is going to transpire. And the other face of Christ, likewise depicted in the account of the events, which take place in the Garden of Olives, regarding which St. John the Evangelist notes: "Jesus, knowing everything that was going to happen . . ." (Jn 18:4).

The great majority of present-day exegetes opt for the Jesus of St. Matthew and explain the sentence of St. John by means of a type of theological identification between the historical Jesus and the Son of God, God himself, confessed by the Christian community sixty years after the death of Jesus. This identification would rule out seeing in the statement of St. John a reflection of the concrete historical behavior of Jesus of Nazareth.

We have, already, at great length, explained why this way of looking at these passages appears incorrect (cf. above, First Part, chap. I; Second Part, chap. VII). But we had to delay the examination of some texts which, seemingly, constitute an objection to the thesis being defended here. Let us now get right to the heart of this difficulty.

What Follows Are Three Useful and
Really Indispensable Preliminary Remarks

a) The "precomprehension" (*see* Third Part, chap. XI) plays a significant part in the choice that one takes. As has already been said above (pp. 91-94) today's exegete or theologian prefers the Jesus of the Synoptics, the only one who may be truly human, and justifies this choice by historical-critical considerations concerning which we have seen that they are in no way compelling. (Second Part, chap. IX). On the other hand, the fathers of the Church and the theologians of the Middle Ages preferred the Christ of St. John and demonstrated that the Christ of the Synoptics was perfectly reconcilable with the Christ of St. John. They were permeated with what we might call an "ecclesial precomprehension." The Christ to whom they adhered was the one whom the tradition of the Church, expressed in the definitions of the great councils, presented to them. They had the certitude that this tradition was a faithful reflection of Scripture. And it is through this perspective that they sought to resolve the exegetical problems which were being posed to them.

b) As can be seen throughout the course of this study, we placed ourselves deliberately on the level of the latter perspective ("ecclesial precomprehension"). We stated this quite clearly (above, pp. 4-5). But we have, at the same time, the certitude that this perspective is perfectly reconcilable with a thorough, honest, scientific, historical-critical exegesis. Certain fathers of the Church, even the greatest among them, such as St. Augustine, have often given these texts a minimizing or "down-played" interpretation. We have noted this (First Part, chap. II) for the text regarding the lack of awareness of the day of judgment (Mk 13:32). We are endeavoring to avoid this perilous reef.

c) The exegesis presented here will be rational, but not rationalistic. A rationalistic exegete rules out, a priori, any possibility of there being a mystery about Jesus of Nazareth. His divinity is presented entirely as a myth. On the other hand, if one admits, at least on the level of an hypothesis, the historicity of a portrait of Jesus presented in the Fourth Gospel, one probably will find that this portrait presents some noncontradictory connections but connections, never-theless, in tension, and reconcilable only with difficulty for the ordinary man on the street.

We will begin by setting forth the frequently discussed question of the "beatific vision" of Jesus of Nazareth. Did Jesus possess, on this earth, the face-to-face vision of God which constitutes the Blessed state of the saints in heaven? Or, to be more exact, we can pose the question in the fol-lowing form: Did the authors of the New Testament, and in particular St. John, think that Jesus, on earth, saw God as the Blessed enjoying eternal life see him? Starting at this point, we will ask ourselves if the conception of these in-spired authors corresponded to the historical situation of Jesus of Nazareth. Finally, we will try to determine the different levels of the knowledge of Jesus, and we will have the necessary instruments at our disposal to study the texts which speak about the ignorance of Jesus or attribute to him some opinions which are apparently false.

Once again, we will not attempt to conceal the precom-prehension underlying this research: "an ecclesial pre-comprehension," which we considered in an earlier section. Anyhow, a precomprehension does exist, whether it is clearly set forth or whether it is unwitting or camouflaged as all those, who have studied the process of historical knowledge, recognize (cf. above, chap. I, pp. 4-5). The precomprehension adopted here, at least, has the advantage of being clearly manifested. But the exegete must obviously be careful to accept the fact that this precomprehension may eventually be called into question by the honest, historical, scientific, critical study of biblical texts (which can only be done if this precomprehension is clearly recog-nized).

2 Did Jesus of Nazareth see God as the saints enjoying eternal life see him?

a The problem

The response to the question raised is: yes, according to the entire tradition since the Middle Ages and probably from the time of St. Augustine.[1] Certainly this is not a matter of a truth of faith. The opposite opinion is only described as an "opinion which cannot be taught with assurance" in an earlier declaration, and competent authority does not currently seem to insist that it be observed.[2] But the traditional doctrine is taught, without restrictions, in the Encyclical of Pius XII on the *Mystical Body* (1943).[3] It is important to realize that it is scarcely any longer held by today's exegetes.

This question has relevance to the subject being treated here since we cannot fail to ask: If Jesus knew that he was God, how did he know it? We have seen that the response of theologians to this question generally is: He knew it by the beatific vision; he sees God as we will see him in heaven.[4] It does indeed seem that this response may be proper and we would like to show, in a rapid fashion, that there exists a solid basis for it in Scripture.

b The testimony of the Fourth Gospel

Did Jesus of Nazareth, who is presented to us in the Fourth Gospel, have the vision of God which is that of the saints in heaven? It seems that we need to respond affirmatively on the condition that we not look in St. John for the theological precisions of medieval scholasticism.

The following formulation seems to be absolutely incontestable: In the Fourth Gospel, Jesus fully enjoys the knowledge of the Father that the *Verbum* possessed before the Incarnation. Texts are quite numerous on this point. Let us quote the most explicit: "Not that anybody has seen the Father, except the one who comes from God; he has seen the Father" (Jn 6:46). Let us also quote the Prologue: "No one has ever seen God; it is the only Son, who is nearest to the Father's heart who has made him known" (1:18). This text gains all of its impact when we recall that it is responding to a text from Ben Sirach which, while speaking of God, demands, "Who has seen him and who would be able to reveal him"? (Sirach 43:31),[5] while understanding: no one. John responds: yes, Jesus. He has seen him and he reveals him. Let us quote once again: "I am telling what I have seen and heard from my Father" (Jn 8:38); "He who comes from heaven bears witness to the things he has seen and heard" (3:32). On the other hand, for John, Jesus, on earth, continued to benefit from this knowledge of the Father which he enjoyed before his Incarnation since everything that he is on earth he continues to be in heaven: "It is the only Son who is in the Father's bosom" (1:18); and he continues to see the Father: "The Son can do nothing by himself. He can only do what *he sees* the Father doing" (5:19).

But, let us recall what has been explained at great length (First Part, chap. I, and Second Part, chap. VII, paragraph 3). The author of the Fourth Gospel is convinced that the Jesus, whom he is describing, is the true Jesus of history (cf. pp. 9-14) and this conviction is sustained, in the eyes of the historian, by testimonies worthy of acceptance (above, pp. 63-67). If the reader is convinced by what has been explained in these two chapters, he must necessarily conclude that the texts, which we have just cited, correspond quite well to what Jesus said and thought about himself. Jesus claimed to enjoy the knowledge of the Father that he had from all eternity, before his Incarnation, and which he continues to enjoy in his present state as son of Mary.

We can say no more, and strictly speaking, we are not dealing with the vision of God which the elect in heaven have, and which is never compared with the knowledge of Jesus. But this knowledge which Jesus has of the Father is, according to the Fourth Gospel, the knowledge of the son of Mary, a knowledge of a man with a human intelligence. Therefore, it should be able to be compared with the different knowledges of God possible for man mentioned in Scripture: knowledge of God by reason; knowledge by faith; prophetic knowledge, product of a special revelation of God; knowledge, finally, which will be that of heaven wherein the elect will see God face to face (for this last type of knowledge cf. Mt 5:8; 1 Cor 13:12; 1 Jn 3:2; Rv 22:4). But only this latter knowledge appears to correspond to the content of the texts of St. John.[6]

c *The testimony of other books of the New Testament*

The other books of the New Testament only present negative testimony on the subject matter of the question which concerns us but it is of tremendous value: It is never a question of the *faith* of the Christ. Certainly, for more than 100 years some exegetes have wanted to interpret, in this manner, some texts in which it was really a question, grammatically speaking, of the faith *of* Jesus. These are the three texts of St. Paul: Galatians 2:20; Romans 3:22 and 3:26. In spite of repeated attempts, the opinion of these exegetes has never been able to take hold.[7] The context really calls for understanding faith *in* Jesus Christ, that which is altogether standard in Greek, in the same way as in English the love of God can signify either man's love of God or God's love of man.

The fact that mention is never made of the faith of Jesus is altogether remarkable, all the more so since Jesus' faith and face-to-face vision of God are not irreconcilable if we take faith in the sense that it so frequently has in the Bible: confidence, surrender, self-abandonment to God. In fact, the Epistle to the Hebrews speaks of the faithful Jesus (*pistos*, Heb 3:2 and 3:5), but not of the faith of Jesus, even though Chapter 11 would be the place for this since it is the conclusion of the panegyric regarding the faith of the saints of the Old Testament. In the same way, the other authors of the New Testament, who so often speak of faith, avoid applying this word to Jesus, when it would have been so easy to do so, and when such a mention would have been, as it were, called for by the context. Why? Isn't the answer found in St. Paul who describes faith in 2 Cor 5:6-7 as the state of someone who "lives in exile far from the Lord," and which is contrasted with "clear sight"? Do not all of these authors of the New Testament instinctively feel, that such is not the condition of Jesus of Nazareth on this earth?

d *The analogy of creative intuition in art*

In the data of Scripture, we have been face-to-face with the classical theological doctrine: During his earthly life, Jesus possessed the vision of God which is that of the elect in heaven. The result appears to be the following: This doctrine is not explicitly attested to by the New Testament; but if we at least admit that the portrait of Jesus drawn in the Fourth Gospel corresponds to historical reality, it seems to be the most satisfying theological systematization of the biblical evidence.[8]

But we have to add a very important detail for the sake of precision. This vision is purely intuitive. It is not being expressed by concepts; in short, it is incommunicable. This is not merely a question of a standard thesis in theology,[9] but of a reality about which there is clear attestation. When Paul speaks of the visions with which the Lord had favored him—which, however, are quite inferior to this beatific vision—he employs an almost contradictory expression: *arreta remata*, some unpronounceable words (2 Cor 12:4). Similarly, the mystics, raised by God to the highest point of contemplation, recognize themselves as being totally incapable of translating that which they were contemplating into any known language.

Here we find ourselves in the face of an apparently insurmountable obstacle. On the one hand, this vision of God is incommunicable and, on the other hand, it is the vision of God which Jesus is communicating (Jn 1:18; 3:32; 8:38). The solution ought to be sought, it seems, in the far-fetched but very real analogy of created intuition in art.[10] Be he an artist of genius: a musician, a painter, a sculptor, a poet, he has an intuition which is incommunicable, incapable of being formulated, even by himself. He sets himself, however, to work, irresistibly pushed or led by the force of this intuition. The work which he will produce will only be a pale reflection of this perception and he will sorrowfully sense the inadequacy of his work of art. However, the work of art is certainly the product of this intuition; and, by groping, he will be able to correct, to modify, whatever in its realization seems clearly to betray his initial perception.

This analogy, which we have already described as being very far-fetched, very imperfect, allows a representation, in the most exaggerated fashion, to be made regarding the duality which characterizes the human intelligence of the Lord. On the one hand, his intelligence as man functioning like our own, but without the blemishes and weaknesses, products of sin; on the other hand, his vision of God, unspeakable, uncommunicable, in which he perceives his humanity united indissolubly to God through the unity of one single divine person, the Son; a mystery, the formulation of which he is able to express in his language as Man, is merely an approximation, undoubtedly true, but a deficient and poor formulation nonetheless. What, by his words and his actions, he will teach to men will only be a pale reflection of the inexpressible splendor which he contemplates.[11]

Certainly, we run a risk in accepting such a portrait, and we are tempted to reject it by saying that such a Jesus is no longer like to his brothers in everything except sin (Heb 2:17 and 4:15). However, the analogy which we have investigated—that of the artistic genius—perhaps allows us to get beyond the difficulty by being more specific about what has been said previously (Third Part, chap. XI): a genius remains a man like us, whether he is a genius in the field of art, the mind, or holiness. But, who will contest the fact that Jesus was indeed a genius? A non-Christian will say—a great religious genius; a person who believes in him will say—the greatest religious genius. Why not place him at the pinnacle of a pyramid on which all men can be located, the higher levels of which would be made up of exceptional men? Would he be less a man for all of that?

Let us finally point out that, according to the very testimony of the Gospel, Jesus possessed what theologians call an "acquired knowledge," the product of an education, of a teaching, of an experience, and which normally developed, as it does in all men, with age, encounters, events: "Jesus grew in knowledge and wisdom and grace before God and man" (Lk 2:52). It is this knowledge which he constantly utilized when the needs of his mission did not demand the employment of a higher knowledge.

3 Various examples of Jesus' ignorance. The minor texts.

Let us now look at the principal texts which would seem to contradict the affirmation: Jesus was God, and he knew it. In this paragraph we will examine some texts which do not present serious objections and in the paragraphs which follow, some texts which we can profitably dwell upon for a longer time.

a The episode of the rich young man according to St. Mark (Mk 10:18)

Jesus responded to the young man who called him "good master": "Why do you call me good? No one is good except God alone." On the level of a statement of the historical Jesus, this text poses no difficulty. All recognize that Jesus, even while possessing perfect awareness of being God, could and even had to speak to the young man by situating himself on the level on which his teaching to the crowds and his activity for them was customarily situated: He intervened as the legate of God charged with announcing the coming of the kingdom and the conditions for entering it. Yet, some will insist: Mark certainly would not have transmitted this sentence if he had the conviction that Jesus was God. The question seems improperly posed. First of all, if, as is likely, this sentence was carried along by the earliest tradition, it was normal that Mark receive it such as it was. Moreover, Mark very strongly affirms that Jesus is the Son of God: this is the very title of his Gospel (Mk 1:1). But in his vocabulary, as in that of the majority of the authors of the New Testament, God is the Father and Jesus is the Son of God. An *explicit* confession of Jesus as God was still premature; time was needed before people could clearly affirm this without appearing to be abandoning the monotheistic faith of the Old Testament. During a long period of time, as has been explained at length (Second Part, chap. VII), this faith existed, but without such a type of formulation which ran the risk of producing misunderstandings and errors. Such surely would have been the situation at the time in which Mark wrote; thus he could have collected this statement without its becoming a problem for him and for his readers. In the same way, we would be able to say that John did not believe that Jesus is God because he cites Jesus saying to his Father: "Eternal life is that they know you, and you the *one* true God" (Jn 17:3)! But, as we have seen, John explicitly confesses the divinity of Christ: (Jn 1:1; 20:28). But in John 17:3 as in Mark 10:18, there is need to affirm, with great conviction, the fidelity of Jesus and of the Christian community to the monotheistic faith of Israel,

so solemnly proclaimed by Christ in his quotation from
Deuteronomy 6:4 and in Mark 12:29.

b The cure of the woman suffering from hemorrhages

She is cured by touching the garment of Jesus, who
asks: "Who has touched my garments"? (Mk 5:30 and
Lk 8:45). These evangelists do not seem to see any contradiction between this question, which supposes a lack of
knowledge, and a knowledge in Jesus of future events,
unforeseen in themselves (the denial of Peter, etc.). Certainly, the evangelists thought that this extraordinary
knowledge was at his disposal, that he used it, not arbitrarily,
but to suit the needs of his ministry. This was also the case
with regard to the miracles; his power to multiply bread
did not prevent him from buying bread in the bakery. This
way of perceiving things on the part of the evangelists was
certainly in conformity with historical reality.

c Jesus' lack of knowledge concerning the Bible

The same explanation provides an understanding of
those texts in which Jesus seems, from the biblical point of
view, to be making mistakes. The supernatural knowledge
of Jesus was not intended to rectify the possibly imperfect
and perhaps erroneous ideas of his hearers about an area
without importance for his mission as Savior. In this area
Jesus spoke in accordance with humanly acquired information, which bore all the limitations of being time bound.
This explains his attribution of Psalm 110 to David (Mk 12:36;
Mt 22:43; Lk 20:42), the use of episodes from the book of
Jonah as if historical events were at issue here (Mt 12:39-41
and 16:4; Lk 11:29-32). In this instance we are dealing with
two opinions very strongly contested by modern exegesis.
Similarly, the slight inaccuracies in Mark 2:26 (Aviatar
instead of Ahimelek) in Matthew 23:35 (Barachia instead
of Jehoyada).

4 The "mistakes" of Jesus concerning the imminence of the end of the world

The following is a very widespread opinion among
many modern exegetes: Jesus announced the future end of

the world as being very close at hand—not extending beyond the duration of a single generation. *He was deceived.* The texts which are the basis of this affirmation are Matthew 10:23 in which Jesus says to his disciples who have been sent forth on mission: "Amen I say to you, the Son of Man comes"; Mark 9:1: "Amen I say to you, there are some present here who will not taste death before having seen the Kingdom of God coming with power" (cf. Lk 9:27; Mt 16:28).

However, the best explanation by far of these texts is the one which sees here the announcement of the Paschal mystery: the Passion-Resurrection-Ascension, Pentecost. Such was the opinion of the founder of the École Biblique, Fr. Lagrange, in his commentary on St. Mark. For it is by means of the Paschal mystery that the kingdom of God has come in all truth. The end of the world will only serve to manifest what was really present, acting with power, but perceptible only through the eyes of faith. A very simple comparison should help our understanding of this. Suppose that someone comes to my room while I am sleeping to bring me a magnificent gift. At what moment did the gift arrive? When he brought it to me during the night or when I woke up and I saw it?

Far from being erroneous, then, these words of Jesus express a profound truth which cuts through the entire Gospel of St. John: eternal life, that of the world to come, that of the eternal kingdom is already present since Easter: "He who believes . . . in eternal life . . . he has passed from death to life" (Jn 5:24). And the Epistle to the Ephesians already affirms this: With Christ, the Father has raised us and made us sit in the heavens through Christ Jesus" (Eph 2:6).

5 Ignorance regarding the day of judgment (Mk 13:32)

Since we are dealing here with a text quoted several times in the course of this work, we are not going to dwell on it overly much. After all that has been explained, it no longer poses a problem. It is a question of the Son, and it is Jesus, the son of Mary, who is speaking and using his intelligence as man. There is no difficulty in admitting that he was really ignorant of the day of judgment in his human knowledge, while, at the same time, totally enjoying the vision of God which is that of the saints in heaven (see, above, 2). Let us now quote from a Thomistic theologian of undisputed competence, Fr. M. J. Nicholas, O.P.:

> It is possible to accord to the psychology of Christ his full humanity, his liberty, his movements, and even his ignorance and his gropings, while holding the great idea, which is the one truly worthy of God-Man, of a direct and intuitive vision of his divinity by his humanity. This is sufficient to extricate us from an identification that everyone seems to make, without seeking to criticize it, between the vision of the divine essence and the vision of all things in it. But this identification doesn't present any necessity. The constant doctrine of St. Thomas is that even all the blessed not only do not see with equal perfection the divine essence, but that they do not see all things, all persons and all events in its light. It is not even merely according to the measure of their charity that they are permitted to see in God this or that, but according to whether or not this or that is of concern to them.[12]

Therefore, through the vision of God, Christ in his humanity saw and knew everything which concerned him, his person, his mission. And God in his wisdom had decided that the knowledge of the day of judgment did not form part of what the man Jesus had to know in order to accomplish his mission. And this is why he was ignorant about this day.

From the biblical point of view, we could, however, offer an objection to this solution. Isn't there a contradiction between this statement regarding his ignorance in Mark 13:32 and the words of Jesus in the Fourth Gospel which presupposed that Jesus had, at his disposal, the divine knowledge of the eternal Son who clearly was not ignorant of anything? (cf. Jn 8:38: "What I, for my part, speak of is what I have seen with my Father.") It is important to answer that, actually, Jesus of Nazareth has, at his disposal, the knowledge which he possesses insofar as being the Word of God, equal to the Father. But nothing says that he had, at his disposal, *all* the knowledge of the *Verbum*. There is a *limitation* clearly expressed in John 15:15: "I have made known to you everything I have learned from my Father." Therefore, what Jesus makes known to his disciples is limited.

6 "Abba, Father, everything is possible for you. Take this cup away from me. But let it be as you, not I, would have it" (Mk 14:36)

It is in the Garden of Gethsemane, at the foot of the Mount of Olives, that Jesus utters this prayer, immediately before his arrest. Mark notes that Jesus made this same prayer several times (14:39) in fright, anguish, and in mortal sadness (14:33ff).

We could apply to this text what we said (Third Part, chap. XII) on the real nature of the sufferings of Christ during his Passion. But this text will be considered from the aspect of the perfect knowledge which Christ possessed regarding his person, his mission, and its fulfillment: Passion, Crucifixion, Resurrection, Glorification.

It is true that this text poses a difficulty. There is in it a problem which Maldonatus[13] strongly emphasized in a text cited and commented upon by Fr. Lebreton[14]: "Jesus spoke as if he were a man to whom the divine will had been only imperfectly known, and as one who didn't have enough strength to overcome death."

In this quote, it is important to point out the "as if," since the evangelists who quote this statement have, some verses previously, also quoted the words of Jesus in the Cenacle announcing the imminence of his Passion and death (Mt 26:28ff; Mk 14:24ff; Lk 22:15-20); thus, in their eyes, there exists no contradiction between the prayer of Jesus at Gethsemane and his words at the Last Supper in which he tells his disciples that it is the last time that he will dine with them and that he is going to die for them. Thus, it is not a question of the ignorance of Jesus which is being taken note of in this text. It is something else and something more mysterious which we can examine on several levels.

On the first level, this prayer expresses the desire of the spontaneous will, the natural inclination of the will of man which is opposed, with all of its strength, to suffering and to death so contrary to his most fervent vow: "that this chalice pass from me." But this natural desire of the spontaneous will clashes with the divine will which *Jesus knew and made his own* through his *free* will which enjoined his *spontaneous* will: "not what I want, but what you want."[15] This is the explanation which St. Thomas Aquinas[16] so clearly presents.

But this distinction, as clear as it may be, is not sufficient to explain the mystery of the Holy Agony of Jesus in Gethsemane. Let us recall the statement of Maldonatus quoted by Fr. Lebreton: "Jesus spoke as if he were a man to whom the divine will had been only imperfectly known and as one who didn't have enough strength to overcome death." This explanation regarding the sadness onto death, the fright and the anguish, derives all of its meaning from what was mentioned a few verses before (Mk 14:33-34). As was said above (Third Part, chap. XII, pp. 98-99), only the saints who Jesus had invited to share in his agony in order to collaborate with him and in him through him in the salvation of the world, can shed some light on this matter. They explain to us how the certitude of the presence of God and of the omnipotence of his love finds refuge in the most inaccessible pinnacle of the soul, entirely submerged in weakness, anguish, sadness, and doubt. This far-fetched analogy allows us to catch a glimpse of how deeply Jesus wanted to identify himself with his brothers in distress by partaking of their trials in order to be for them a model and an example. But, above all, they help us to understand how Jesus "had been made sin for us," "became a curse for us" (2 Cor 5:21; Gal 3:13). Jesus wanted to place himself in solidarity with sinful humanity by sharing not in the sin but in its consequences: weakness, doubt, sadness, anguish, distancing from God. But this solidarity had, as its goal, the transformation of humanity destined for death by infusing his own divine life, his risen life into it.

We can merely look again at the beautiful pages which have been devoted to the Holy Agony by Fr. Lebreton, who was himself a true mystic[17] and a very great historian of early Christianity, whose scientific competence was highly regarded by all. The pages devoted to Gethsemane are of unparalleled depth; we perceive in them the spiritual experience of a real man of God. These pages show better than anything which has been attempted, in these few lines, the real nature of the scene at Gethsemane. This episode is in no way opposed to what has been said regarding the perfect knowledge which Jesus had of his person, of his Father and of the mission received from him. On the contrary, this scene really takes shape by virtue of this knowledge which Jesus had about himself and his redemptive mission.

7 "My God, my God, why have you abandoned me"? (Mt 27:46 and Mk 15:34)

We can treat this text in a much more rapid fashion: the essential point has already been made in the preceding paragraph. This cry of Jesus is only the expression of his agony in the Garden of Olives but now pushed to the highest limit and degree of sorrow and suffering.

One point should first of all be clear, even though it has been often questioned: Jesus quotes the first verse of Psalm 22. Actually, if Jesus had wanted merely to express a personal prayer without reference to the psalm he would have said: "My Father" for Jesus never prayed "My God" apart from this single text. And the very fact that he twice repeats: "My God," a repetition, moreover, without any parallel in the prayer of Jesus, is even more of an argument. Jesus quotes Scripture.

This does not mean that Jesus is not making this prayer his own. But it invites us to understand this cry in the context of the entire psalm. Let us indicate that Jesus said it in Aramaic, which implies a certain personal familiarity with this psalm since, in the liturgy, it was recited in Hebrew: now, as a matter of fact, and this is the second point, the liturgy infrequently used this psalm. The earliest testimonies regarding this relate to the Feast of Purim in which the deliverance of the Jews of Persia, who were destined for extermination by Haman, is celebrated. Psalm 22 appears to be there at its right place since it is describing a desperate situation, transformed by God into a deliverance.

It is therefore proper to state as strongly as we can: If Jesus had wanted to express a feeling of distress and abandonment without certainty of deliverance, he would not have quoted this psalm, but he would have said: "Father, you are abandoning me. . . ."

The conclusion becomes evident. We are, therefore, not obliged to choose between two contradictory attitudes: Jesus announcing his condemnation, death, and Resurrection; and the crucified Jesus expressing his despair and suffering for having been abandoned by God in a truly irreversible fashion.

Jesus really wanted, on Golgotha as in Gethsemane, to undergo the consequences of the sin which distanced and separated from God—this God whom he continued to contemplate but with a contemplation which does not bring him any joy or comfort, since he was experiencing, in all of its dire force, the opposition between the thrice holy God and the sin of humanity which he wished to assume.

In beholding the divine holiness, Isaiah cried out: "Woe is me, I am lost, for I am a man of unclean lips and I live among a people of unclean lips and my eyes have looked at the King, Yahweh Sabaoth" (Is 6:5). These sentiments of the prophet only offer a feeble idea of what the heart of Jesus was experiencing; this abandonment, which he was suffering, was the abandonment by God to which sinful humanity was condemned and which he had come to heal. It was also this apparent abandonment which so many innocent victims of the sin of the world experience, this absence of the God of love which seems to be hidden when man suffers and is tortured. Jesus wanted to experience all of this in order to transform it ultimately into joy which knows no end, the joy of Easter.

Conclusion

THE REAL HISTORICAL JESUS

Is he at the beginning or the end of gospel tradition?

At the conclusion of this study, let us briefly review the area which we have covered.

The initial question was the following: Would Jesus of Nazareth recognize himself in the words which the Fourth Gospel places in his mouth: "Before Abraham was, I am"; "Father, give me the glory that I had with you before the world began"?

In the First Part, we showed that throughout the entire unanimous Christian tradition and in different churches, the affirmative response to this question was accepted up until a relatively recent period; that, at the beginning of this tradition there was, in the Fourth Gospel, a clear will to transmit the following doctrine by contrasting it with those (Judeo-Christians, etc.) who did not admit it: Jesus is God, and if we believe it, it is because he himself has said it. And we have concluded that the unanimity in this tradition expressed the *faith* of the Church.

A Second Part had, as its purpose, to show the excellent foundation of this doctrine from the point of view of history: Jesus really affirmed that he was God. Thus, the affirmation: "Jesus taught that he was God" was presented as a working hypothesis. And we have reflected on the manner in which Jesus would have used it so that his audience would have accepted this teaching. We have come to realize that a very gradual teaching was called for in this instance; quite allusive for the crowd, more precise for the disciples, and more complete still for the disciples most likely to understand it. We have compared this a priori process with what the historical-critical study of the gospel tradition reveals; this comparison has, a posteriori, proven the initial working hypothesis.

In the course of the inquiry, a quasi form of evidence appeared: The doctrine of the divinity of Jesus was certainly already established in Christian communities around the year 50. Its appearance therefore obviously sprung up some years before. Now this is a period in which the evangelization of the pagan world had just about begun; every active and dynamic element came from Judaism. In Judaism, at this time, there was a gut-level horror of anything which recalled or alluded to the divinization of great men, so frequent in detested paganism. This horror must have absolutely ruled out the possibility of any invention of the doctrine affirming the divine nature of Jesus. Such an obstacle could only be surmounted by incontestable certitude. Only an explicit teaching of Jesus, confirmed by the miracle of Easter, fulfilled this condition.

Finally, in the Third Part, we attempted to respond to several objections arising from a precomprehension stemming from the world in which we live: Jesus is no longer truly man if he knows that he is God and if he knows his future in detail. We have shown that such a problem was totally foreign to the fathers of the Church, to the doctors of the Middle Ages, to the early reformers, and above all to the evangelists. Do we really know, better than they, what a man is? We made one final effort to give an existential context to the gospel affirmation: "Before Abraham was, I am"; and to do this we had recourse to the far-fetched but real analogy which the experience of certain mystics offers.

Finally, we endeavored to resolve the problem posed by certain texts which, at first sight, seem to contradict the doctrine being defended here. These texts, on the contrary, explained in the framework of this doctrine, allow for a much deeper understanding of the psychology of Jesus who in order to save us, assumes not sin itself but its most painful consequences.

At the conclusion of this attempt, let us extend the debate and return to the problem of method in Christology, a problem which has been so often mentioned in these pages.

For more than eighty years, the question studied here has been clarified by the truly profound remarks of Maurice Blondel. Let us look once again at the lengthy section which we quote (above, p. 80). To the best of our knowledge the point of view presented in these lines has not been contested by anyone since it is so clear. But we can, however, say that it has, to a large extent, been greatly ignored.

If we admit, and it would only be as a working hypothesis, that Jesus of Nazareth was indeed the one whom St. John presents to us: the *Verbum* who is God and who incarnated himself in order to save mankind; if we admit, always in the context of the same working hypothesis, that Jesus was fully aware both of this mystery and of his mission of making it known to men, then it would appear evident that this mystery could not be revealed, straight off to men, formed by a mentality so little in agreement with such a doctrine. There was need for a long period of maturation, a pedagogy which would be attentive to presenting, along each step of the way, what could be assimilated by an audience which was so little receptive, while at the same time, reserving to a more intimate circle a number of more explicit revelations. And these revelations themselves could only be spread beyond this group at a time when the events of Easter and the sending of the Spirit at Pentecost would have made the disciples more receptive to what, at the beginning, they would have shunned and recoiled from with such great horror.

Obviously, it is possible to reduce the Jesus of history to what the earliest witnesses transmitted with their prejudices, their narrowness, and their expectations, so little conformed to what Jesus came to bring. But then we, a priori, dismiss the evidence that there was a mystery of Jesus which shatters all the categories and structures by which the mind-set of this period was locked in.

On the other hand, if we admit that this mystery exists and that Jesus knew it, we admit as self-evident that it is at the *end* of the gospel tradition and not at its point of departure that the real personality of Jesus of Nazareth—son of Mary and Son of God, who trod the same paths as we and who showed us that he existed before the creation of the world in a glory identical to that of the Father—will be revealed.

We have attempted to show, in a scientifically convincing fashion, that such was actually the very purpose of the Fourth Gospel: to present the real Jesus of Nazareth such as he was in reality, Son of Man and Son of God, God himself, knowing that he was and saying it.

And we have shown that, from the point of view of the historian, we have excellent reasons for believing that he was not deceived.

In short, we have tried to show that, from the point of view of rigorous and honest historical-critical exegesis, we have no reason for rejecting or doubting the figure of the Jesus of history which the Fourth Gospel, the fathers of the Church, the ecumenical councils and the unanimous testimony of almost twenty centuries of Christian tradition, present to us. If in the course of his earthly life, Jesus would have had the Fourth Gospel between his hands, he would have said: It is, indeed, I.

Endnotes

Preface

1. Raymond E. Brown, S.S., *Jesus, God and Man* (Milwaukee, 1968), p. 86.
2. P. Benoit, "La divinité de Jésus," in *Lumière et Vie*, (no. 9, 1953), p. 45, or *Exegese et Theologie*, I (Paris, 1961), p. 118. English: "The Divinity of Jesus in the Synoptic Gospels" in *Jesus and the Gospels* (London: Longman and Todd, 1943), vol. I, p. 48.
3. J. A. T. Robinson, *Peut-on se fier au Nouveau Testament?* Paris, 1980, p. 18; original English text: "Fundamentalism of the Fearful," with a play on words between faithful and fearful, in *Can We Trust the New Testament?* (Grand Rapids: 1977), p. 16.
4. J. Lebreton, "Le désaccord entre la foi populaire et la théologie savante dans l'Eglise chrétienne du IIIe siecle," *Rev. d'Hist. Ecclés.*, 19 (1923), 481-505 and 20 (1924), 5-37, summarized in *Histoire de l'Eglise* under the direction of A. Fliche et V. Martin, tome II (Paris, 1935), pp. 361-74. (English: *The History of the Primitive Church* (London: Burns and Oates, 1948), II, ch. XIV, par. 2).

Introduction

1. I intentionally did not repeat the exact title of the book. For "Did Jesus Know that He was God" implies that we have already answered yes to the question "Is Jesus God"? This question depends on faith and not on historical investigation, although historical investigation can furnish certain elements for a response.
2. One will remark that the first hypothesis excludes 2 and 3; the latter two hypothesis, on the other hand, can be true at the same time.
3. On the subject of historical knowledge and on precomprehension, we can consult: H. I. Marrou, *De La Connaissance historique*, 7 ed. (Paris: 1975), pp. 26-63; R. Bultmann, "Das Problem der Hermeneutik," *Zeitschr, für Theologie und Kirche* (1950), 205-12.

Chapter I

1. St. Justin, *Dialogue with Trypho* 48:4; 49:1; St. Irenaeus *Adversus Haereses*, I:26 (Cerinthus and the Ebionites); St. Hippolytus, *Philosophoumena*, VII, 33.

2. St. Irenaeus, *Adversus Haereses*, III, 11:1; on Cerinthus. ibid., I, 26:1, quoted by St. Hippolytus (cf. preceding note).

3. St. Jerome, Prologue to the *Commentary on the Gospel of St. Matthew*, PL 26, col. 19.

4. Raymond E. Brown, *Jesus, God and Man* (Milwaukee: 1968), p. 92.

5. The Constitution *Dei Verbum* on Revelation, ch. 5, no. 19: "Indeed, after the Ascension of the Lord, the Apostles handed on to their hearers what he had said and done, this they did with that clear understanding which they enjoyed after they had been instructed by the glorious events of Christ and taught by the Spirit of Truth."

6. Merely refer to the principal commentaries on the Fourth Gospel. Confer, for example, the Ecumenical Translation of the Bible, *Nouveau Testament, edition integrale* (Paris, 1972), pp. 286-87; *Bible de Jerusalem* in one volume, 2nd edition (Paris: 1973), pp. 1523-1527 (M.-E. Boismard).

7. "The work of John would remain incomprehensible if we choose to deny that he was convinced of the historical reality of the events which he was recounting," M.-E. Boismard, op. cit. (cf. preceding note), p. 1525.

Chapter II

1. St. Irenaeus, *Adv. Haeres.*, II, 28:6-8; Origen, *in Matth.*, PG 13, col. 1686ff. But Origen presents another more "widespread" opinion: he states: Christ speaks in the name of the Church.

2. See the very precise study of J. Lebreton, *History of the Dogma of the Trinity*, I (London: Burns and Oates, 1939). Appended Note C, Mark 13:34, The Ignorance of the Day of Judgment. These authors think that Jesus as man really knew the day of judgment; among the better known fathers, Hilary, Ambrose, Chrysostom, Augustine, Didymus, Epiphanius, Basil of Caesarea; but there are also a great number of others who are less well known. During the Middle Ages, it became the common opinion among the scholastics.

3. Thus Fr. Lagrange, *Èvangile de Saint Marc*, 4th ed. (1928), on Mark 13:32.

4. Thus St. Irenaeus (above, note 1); Gregory of Nyssa. But a large number of fathers admit the two interpretations: Athanasius, Basil, Gregory of Nazianzen, etc. We can apply to these fathers what

Lebreton said of St. Athanasius (op. cit., p. 563): "The entire effort of St. Athanasius attempts to establish that the Divine *Verbum* is ignorant of nothing; by comparison with this most important affirmation, everything else is for him of little importance and he proposes several different interpretations of the Gospel text: ignorance set aside by the divinity of Christ and attributed to his humanity is presented at one time as apparent, and at another time, as real."

5. H. Denzinger—A. Schonmetzer, *Enchiridion symbolorum et declarationum*, 32nd ed. (Fribourg en B.: 1963), no. 295 (in what follows abbreviated as *DS*).

6. St. Augustine seems to have taught that in the course of his earthly life Jesus saw God face-to-face, like the saints in heaven: *De diversis quaestionibus*, 60:65, PL 40, col. 60. On the question of the human knowledge of Christ according to St. Augustine, we will consult T. J. Van Bavel, *Recherches sur la christologie de S. Augustin*, (Fribourg, Switzerland: 1954), pp. 146-75. The treatment of A.-M. Dubarle, "La science humaine du Christ d'après S. Augustin," *Rev. Sc. Phil. Theol.*, 29 (1940), 244-64, appears more questionable.

7. DS, no. 419.

8. PL 65, col. 415.

9. Ibid., col. 420-23.

10. Ibid., col. 417ff. St. Fulgentius does not indicate according to what manner Christ, in his human intelligence, was aware of his divine nature. He only says that it is by the action of the Spirit which is given to him without limitation, and therefore it is not by the strength of his own human intelligence.

11. DS, nos. 301-2.

12. Alcuin, *De fide S. Trinitatis*, III, 11, PL 101, col. 30; Hugh of St. Victor, *De sapientia animae Christi*, PL 176, col. 845.

13. See J. Lebreton, *Histoire du dogme de la Trinité des origines au Concile de Nicee*, t. I, *Les Origines*, 6th edit. (paris, 1927), pp. 581-86, with the indication of sources and of important works on this question (cf. note 2, above).

14. DS, 475.

15. St. John Damascene, *Book of Heresies*, 85, PG 94, col. 756.

16. St. John Damascene, *De fide orthodoxa*, III, 19, PG 94, col. 1080.

Chapter III

1. Thus the *Summa Sententiarum*, for a long time attributed to Hugh of St. Victor (who died in 1140), observes: "It is important to state without any hesitation that in Christ there wasn't any other knowledge than divine knowledge" (*Summa Sententiarum*, I, 16, PL 176, col. 74). The Franciscan, Alexander of Hales (who died in 1245) admits six

areas of knowledge in Christ: divine knowledge, the knowledge of "union" (corresponding to the union in Jesus of his humanity and divinity), the knowledge of the beatific vision, and three purely human forms of knowledge (*Summa Theologica*, III, 13). St. Thomas will refute both of these (*Summa Theologica*, III, q. 9, art. 1).

2. Thus St. Albert the Great (*In Sentent.*, III, dist. 13 et 14), St. Bonaventure (*In Sentent.*, III, dist. 14), and above all St. Thomas (*Summa Theologica*, IIIa, q. 9-12).

3. "No one has ever seen God; it is the only Son, who is nearest to the Father's heart, who has made him known." In his commentary on St. John, Fr. Lagrange writes: "This allows us to understand that Jesus enjoyed the beatific vision during this life. The theological thesis seems to us to have here a solid basis." This impression is confirmed if we notice that John is responding affirmatively to the negative question of Sirach (Ecc 43:31): "Who has ever seen him to give a description"? Cf. within p. 22.

4. It is important to note that, on this point, thirteenth-century theologians are not unanimous and that St. Thomas himself successively maintained differing opinions. Cf. C.-V. Héris, *Le Verbe incarné* (St. Thomas, *Summa Theologica*, ed. de la "Revue des Jeunes"), Volume II, IIIa, q. 7 to 15 (Paris-Tournai-Rome: 1927), p. 324, explanatory note 49. It is important to note that this infused knowledge is, as St. Thomas says, "univocally similar to our own" (IIIa, q. 11, art. 5, *sed contra*). For man in the state of grace, it is the knowledge of the gifts of the Holy Spirit (wisdom, knowledge, understanding) and the charisms (IIIa, q. 11, art. 1, corp.).

5. IIIa, q. 9, art. 1, ad 1; St. Thomas reacts against the opinion of the theologians mentioned in note 1.

6. IIIa, q. 10, a. 4, corpus.

7. St. Thomas says that, by his infused knowledge, Jesus *knows* all the mysteries which are the object of Revelation (IIIa, q. 11, a. 1, corp.). He knows them, like the prophets, with a sure knowledge, but with a certitude of *faith*. This would be especially the case with respect to his own divine nature. He would have to make an act of faith in his divinity; cf. within, note 10, the quotation of Fr. Garrigou-Lagrange.

8. Such is the position of K. Rahner, *Probleme der Christologie von neute en Schriften zur Theologie* #I (Köln: Benzinger, 1962), pp. 190-91; of J. Mouroux, *Le Mystere du temps* (Paris: 1962), pp. 100-20; and some others.

9. IIIa, q. 9, a. 1, the third objection, and his response. After the Council of Chalcedon, the divine nature and the human nature coexist in Christ without mixture or confusion. Consequently, Thomists declare there isn't any proper action of God, the *Verbum*, on the humanity of Christ. The *divine action* on the humanity of Christ depends on the divine *nature* and it is common to the three Persons.

10. Thus V. Héris, "A propos d'un article sur la psychologie du Christ," *Rev. Sc. Ph. Theol.*, 43 (1959), 462-71. *See* 468-71. But he specifies on page 471, that only the beatific vision allows Jesus "to grasp without any shadow" his divine personality. Without the beatific vision, Jesus actually had to "Believe, obscurely," in his divinity as Fr. Garrigou-Lagrange correctly states in *Le Sauveur et son amour pour nous* (Paris: 1933), p. 198.

11. Such is the opinion of Fr. Garrigou-Lagrange, loc. cit. (cf. above, note 10), of J. Maritain, *De la grace et de l'humanité de Jesus* (Paris: 1967), p. 11f. (a position akin to that of Fr. Héris, but more appealing: Jesus had evidence of his divinity through his beatific vision, but the evidence was incommunicable for it was "supraconscious." The infused knowledge allows for the formulation and the communication of it); J.-H. Nicolas, in *Rev. Thomiste*, 53 (1953), 423ff.; and many others.

12. J.-H. Nicolas, loc. cit. (cf. above, note 11), writes: "It is certainly necessary to say that, if it did not possess the beatific vision, the soul of Christ would possess an awareness in itself of a mystery. His awareness would not be shut up upon a human me which did not exist and would be powerless to attain his me which is divine." v. Héris similarly writes: "That is why, as strange as it appears at first sight, it is evident that Christ, by the mere force of his human faculties, was not able to be aware of his divine personality. . . . The sole psychological effect, which may be the result of the hypostatic union, is the perfect moral rectitude or righteousness of Christ. But this result is only indirect: it is based on the fact that God, personally united to the human nature, finds himself committed to safeguarding this nature from every fault by a special efficacious assistance. . . . Christ, experiencing his absolute sinlessness, would have been able to conclude to a totally special benevolence by God with respect to him and to a supremely high moral union of his soul with God, but never would he conclude to the hypostatic union and to the mystery of grace which it implies" (*La Mystère du Christ* (Paris: 1928), p. 84f.

Chapter IV

1. See Vatican Council I, The Constitution *Dei Filius*, I ch. 3 (DS, 3011).

Chapter V

1. To affirm that "everything which the New Testament says on the subject of Jesus corresponds to what Jesus thought of himself" evidently implies that "everything that the New Testament says on the subject of Jesus" constitutes a coherent whole. This latter point

will not be accepted by those who think there is in the New Testament several irreconcilable Christologies. But this opinion is very debatable. That alone is irreconcilable which is contradictory to the precise meaning of the word (A different from A). Now, we don't find any such contradictions in the New Testament affirmations relative to Christ. What we do find there are some tensions between affirmations which appear to be in opposition, not in contradiction. Christian faith likewise affirms that there are three divine persons and one God; it affirms at the same time, grace and freedom, the infinite mercy of God, and the existence of hell, etc. In this instance, it is a fundamental property of the mystery of God and of Christ.

Chapter VI

1. J.-A. Fitzmyer, S.J., *A Christological Catechism, New Testament Answers* (Ramsey: Paulist Press, 1982), p. 84.

2. For the majority of critics, Mark 2:7 had been inserted at a later date, right within the episode of the cure of the paralytic. But very many exegetes quite firmly maintain the historicity of the episode which is reported in Mark 2:5b-10. They think, with adequate reason, that the mere fact of belonging to a later redaction is, in no way, an indication of nonhistoricity. Other arguments are needed.

3. Including R. Bultmann, *Jesus* (Breslin: 1929), pp. 78-79.

4. P. Benoit, "La divinité de Jesus," in *Lumière et Vie*, no. 9 (1953), 51ff. Eng. Edit., (cf. Preface, note 2), pp. 53-54.

5. Some wish to explain these texts by recalling that, according to certain rabbinic traditions, there would have been a changing of the law of Moses, at the time of the Messiah. On this subject we can consult W. Davies, *The Sermon on the Mount* (Cambridge University Press, 1966), pp. 57-63. W. Davies thinks, with adequate reason that apparently these texts are too late, too imprecise to be able to establish such a point of view.

6. Actually, this word of Jesus is also reported in Luke 14:26, according to a formulation which, from the point of view of language, appears more archaic. It is this word which Bultmann cites as an authentic word of Jesus, *Jésus*, op. cit. (cf. note 3), pp. 33, 91.

7. Some times, as a parallel, there is cited: Deuteronomy 33:9, but it is a matter of the service of God; the vocation of Eliseus, I Kings 19:19-20, but what is in question is the priority of a mission, not the preferential attachment to a person. As for the rabbinic texts quoted as parallel (cf. Strack-Billerbeck on this passage), it is a question of an order of precedence with respect to services to be rendered, in which the Master goes before the Father.

8. Regarding this parable, we can refer to X. Leon-Dufour, "Le parabole

des vignerons homicides," *Etudes d'Evangile*, (Paris, 1965), pp. 308-30; and to the work of M. Hubaut, "La parabole des vignerons homicides." *Cahiers de la Revue Biblique*, no. 16 (Paris: 1976), which studies, in greater detail, the problems of authenticity and, by way of review, examines the opinions of critical exegesis. Both are in agreement in attributing the essential of the parable to Jesus himself, in particular the mention of Son.

9. See, for example, the notes in the Jerusalem Bible.

10. Leon-Dufour, op. cit. (cf. note 8), p. 322.

11. See Strack-Billerbeck, vol. III, p. 673, on Hebrews, 1:3.

12. Ecumenical translation of the Bible = T.O.B.

13. Among the modern exegetes who hold for authenticity, let us mention P. Benoit, art. cit., "La divinité de Jesus," *Lumière et Vie*, no. 9, 1953, p. 60; (English text, cf. Preface note 2, p. 60); C. Spicq, *Dieu et l'Homme in the N.T.* (Paris: 1961), pp. 80ff.; L. Cerfaux, *Recueils L. Cerfaux* III (Gemblous, 1962), p. 159; A. Feuillet, "Jésus et la Sagesse divine d'après les évangiles synoptiques" *RB* 62 (1955), 196; X. Leon-Dufour, *Les Èvangiles et l'histoire de Jésus* (Paris: 1963), p. 412; R. E. Brown, *Jesus, God and Man* (Milwaukee: 1968), p. 90 (he adopts the thesis of J. Jeremias, cf. above). Among nonCatholic exegetes: J. Jeremias, *Neutestamentlich Theologie*, (Gutersloh: G. Mohn, I, 1971), pp. 63-65. (he would choose to see as the basis of this a parabolic form: likewise no one knows a father, except a son); O. Cullmann, *The Christology of the New Testament* (London: SCM Press, 1959), pp. 287-88. V. Taylor, *The Names of Jesus* (London: 1953), p. 64; C.-H. Dodd, *The Founder of Christianity* (New York: Macmillan, 1970). Among exegetes of the preceding generation: Lagrange, Huby, Lebreton, etc., and even Albert Schweitzer. The list clearly is far from being exhausted.

14. S. Legasse, "Le logion sur le Fils revelateur (Mt 11:27 and Lk 10:22)," in *La Notion biblique de Dieu*, 13 biblical days of 1974 at the 25th Colloquim *Biblicum Lovaniense*, (Gembloux-Louvain: 1976), pp. 245-74, especially pp. 269-73.

15. Ibid., pp. 271ff. *See also* his criticism of the thesis of Jeremias (cf. note 13), p. 271, [note 133], a justifiable criticism, it would seem.

16. Moreover, we find it difficult to understand the hesitations of S. Legasse, who finally leans toward a creation by the community (p. 273): "The particular stamp of our logion raises some hesitation. With this claim of transcendence, we would prefer to have a supplementary guarantee" (p. 272). Which guarantee? "We would prefer, on another level, to discover the equivalent of Matthew 11:27 in the Synoptics" (ibid.). O. Cullmann provides a good insight when he writes that such a demand is hardly reasonable. "How many pearls contained in the Sermon on the Mount would have to be cast aside as inauthentic if we allowed ourselves to be guided by this principle"! (*Saint Pierre, disciple, apotre et martyr* (Neuchatel-Paris: 1952), p. 154,

with reference to those who reject the authenticity of the logion of Jesus on the primacy of Peter for the same reason.) In a general manner, we will subscribe unreservedly to the very prudent remarks of Fr. Benoit concerning gospel texts which are presented as words of Jesus: "To read many modern critics . . . , we have the impression that the texts are treated as the accused, and not as witnesses. An attitude which is suitable neither to a judge nor to an historian. Rather than listening to the text with sympathy and confidence even if it should be necessary to criticize it and to condemn it if it was known to be at fault, it is approached with an opposite attitude of mistrust and suspicion. This is wrong, a priori, and if someone wishes to maintain that he is right, he bears the burden of proof" (P. Benoit, "Jésus et le Serviteur de Dieu," in *Jesus aux origines de la Christologie*, biblical days of Louvain, 1973 (Gembloux-Louvain: 1975,] pp. 111-40. The quote is on p. 136). In this same article, Fr. Benoit states that very often the authenticity of a word of Jesus is put in doubt when he expresses himself as his contemporaries or the early Christians (principle of "difference"), and moreover, it is debated whether he is the author of an idea or of an expression unknown to the Judaism of his time: "He hasn't the right to speak as the people of his time nor of saying something else. What remains for him except silence? I know of no better way to muzzle a man" (ibid., p. 139).

17. Strack-Billerbeck gives no rabbinical parallel to Matthew 11:27. The Hellenistic parallels presented by Legasse, art. cit. (cf. note 14), p. 265ff., are interesting. But not one speaks of a knowledge which no one else (*oudeis*) would possess. The least far-fetched parallel is in the Old Testament: Numbers 12:7, which speaks of a certain superiority of Moses with respect to the prophets. But it is solely a matter of something transitory or momentary (concerning the moment of prophetic revelation), and related to the manner of the appearance and communication of God, not of a permanent knowledge; and it isn't said explicitly or implicitly that no one knows Yahweh except Moses.

18. S. Legasse, art. cit. (cf. note 14), p. 255.

19. Bibliographical summary: three works of J. Jeremias: *The Prayers of Jesus* (Philadelphia: Fortress Press, 1978), pp. 11-65; *The Central Message of the New Testament* (London: SCM Press, 1965), pp. 9-30; *Neutestamentliche Theologie* (cf. note 13). Two works of W. Marchel *Dieu Pere dans le Nouveau Testament* (Paris: 1966; *Abba, Père, la priere du Christ et des chretiens* (Rome: 1963) (the latter being more technical).

20. Thus Jeremias (cf. note 13: p. 73). In this latter book, Jeremias refuses to draw out from the usage of this word some consequences concerning Christian dogma: preexistence, equality with the Father. But it is important to avoid giving the last word on the meaning of this word. Like the preceding texts, it "gives food for thought" and it is fitting for nourishing the reflection of the disciples.

21. Thus W. Marchel (cf. note 19), *Abba, Père,* pp. 170ff.

Chapter VII

1. M. J. Lagrange, *Èvangile selon saint Jean,* 3rd ed., 1927, p. CLVII; H. Riesenfeld, *The Gospel Tradition and its Beginnings* (London: 1957), p. 28; O. Cullmann, *Le Milieu johannique* (Neuchatel-Paris: 1976), pp. 41, 120, 136.

2. J. Dupont, in the Jerusalem Bible, in Acts 2:21, note reproduced in the edition in one volume. The opinion which sees solely the theology of Luke in these texts is very debatable.

3. *See* Ecumenical Translation of the Bible (T.O.B.) New Testament (Paris: 1972), p. 584.

4. Cf. T.O.B., note on this verse.

5. Cf. T.O.B., note on this verse.

6. M. Hengel, *The Son of God* (Philadelphia: Fortress Press, 1976), pp. 1-20. This author does not in any way take into consideration the hypothesis being set forth here; at the origin of the doctrine of the preexistence and divinity of Christ, there would be a teaching of the historical Jesus. This renders still more valuable his affirmations regarding the extraordinarily rapid spread of the Christology of the preexisting Christ and Son of God.

7. A current in modern exegesis, but still a minority, endeavors to prove that the doctrine of preexistence is not to be found in any text of St. Paul. It would be absent from Philippians, 2:6-11. But the over-whelming majority of exegetes is of a radically different opinion. Moreover one of the most prominent representatives of this minority current, actually very clearly acknowledges this fact. Cf. J. Murphy O'Connor, "Christological Anthropology in Philippians, 2:6-11," in *Revue Biblique* 83 (1976), 25-50. He speaks of the "solid consensus" of exegetes in favor of the presence in Philippians 2:6-11, of the doctrine of the preexistence of Christ (p. 30).

   Having said this, the differences are quite numerous in what concerns the division, the structure, the flow of ideas, the meaning of the most important words. This is not new. It already existed during the patristic period, cf. P. Grelot, "La traduction et l'interpretation de Philippiens 2:6-7. "Quelques elements d'enguête patristique," *Nouv. Revue Theol.* 93 (1971), 897-922 and 1009-1026.

8. Hengel, *The Son of God* (note 6 above), p. 2. Hengel quotes yet another Protestant exegete who is very well known, namely M. Dibelius, who writes that the essential problem in Christology is the question of knowing how the knowledge about the historical personality of Jesus was transformed so rapidly into faith in the heavenly Son of God (*Religion in Geschichte und Gegenwart,* vol. I, 2nd ed., 1927, col. 1593, quoted by Hengel, op. cit., p. 14, n. 1).

9. We have placed between parenthesis the words which are not in the text, and which are necessary for a correct English translation. We know that in Hebrew and in Aramaic the verb to be is generally omitted. As a good Semite, Paul necessarily supplies for the verb to be when he omits the verb.

10. Concerning the affirmation regarding the preexistence of Christ in I Corinthians 8:6, there is the same consensus as for Philippians 2:6-11. This is recognized even by those who hold a different position: "According to a widespread consensus, this passage is recognized as the earliest attestation of the preexistence of Christ" (J. Murphy O'Connor 1 Cor 8:6. "Cosmology or Soteriology"? *Revue Biblique* 85 (1978), 253).

11. For R. Bultmann, *Theology of the New Testament*, 4th ed., 1965, I p. 131ff., 188, 304, the preexistence is supposed in St. Paul in texts such as Romans 8:32; Galatians 4:4, in addition to the three texts studied above: Philippians 2:6-11; 1 Corinthians 8:6; 2 Corinthians 8:9.

12. R. Bultmann, *Theology of the New Testament*, 4th ed. (1965), vol. I, p. 131.

13. M. Hengel, *The Son of God* (note 6 above), pp. 23-41.

14. In the same work of M. Hengel we will find a lengthy analysis of Jewish notions which could have been used by the early Christians in order to aid them in formulating their faith in Jesus, Son of God: *The Son of God*, pp. 41-57; 66ff.

15. This is, however, what was usually stated, during the last few decades, by a great number of exegetes: the origin of faith in the divinity of Christ, impossible in the Palestinian world, was much less so for Christians of Jewish origin, but coming from communities existing outside the Holy Land. They were more capable of being influenced by their pagan environment. This is absolutely indefensible. It is not possible to cite texts coming from non-Palestinian Judaism which are less ferociously anti-idolatrous than those deriving from Jews living in the Holy Land. There is no trace of syncretism, as was once found in the Jewish colony of Elephantine (fifth century before Jesus Christ). Moreover, recent works (S. Liebermann, M. Hengel) have contributed to toning down the line of separation once traditionally admitted between Judaism and the Holy Land and that of the communities situated outside of Palestine. We are better aware today of the situation in the Holy Land at the beginning of the Christian era and we know that the influence of Greek culture was very strong there, even among the Jews.

16. It would be necessary to have experienced for oneself the spiritual journey of a St. Paul in order to measure the enormous difficulty which faith in the mystery of the Incarnation presents for an orthodox Jew. With respect to this, all the other obstacles are ridiculous child's play. This obstacle is so radical that it cannot be surmounted frontally; it must be skirted, like a summit whose northern face is inaccessible

and which can only be scaled from the south. It is only afterward, through the light of faith, that one discovers that the Trinity and the Incarnation are not opposed to the monotheistic dogma of Israel: "Hear O Israel, the Lord our God, the Lord is one" (Mk 12:29 citing Dt 6:4). And one discovers that not only is there no contradiction but on the contrary the Christian dogma is as it were the full blossoming out, the crowning of the faith of Israel. And for someone who has made a similar experience, there is a conviction which comes to bear on the subject: The pious Jew of the first century is in an identical situation to someone of today. Only a very strong certitude can lead him to skirt around this obstacle. Only an indisputable teaching of Jesus fulfills this condition.

17. We are not entering here into the problem of the Son of Man, of his nature, of his preexistence, we wish to remain faithful to our methodology which consists in only relying upon data in which a certain exegetical consensus obtains; but this is certainly not the case for the texts relating to the Son of Man.

18. The historian, by saying that, does not go beyond the limits of his method. He has perhaps not to take a position regarding the reality of the Resurrection (the "perhaps" is intentional, for in my view he can do it). He must certainly testify to the role that this faith in the Resurrection has played in the thought of the early Christians and the consequences that they derived from it: God has authenticated the life, the mission, and the teaching of Jesus of Nazareth.

19. This is the date currently proposed by the majority of exegetes. Some recent discoveries have totally contradicted the thesis of those who want to date the Fourth Gospel around the first half of the second century. But an earlier date remains possible. The Anglican Bishop, J. A. T. Robinson, has proposed A.D. 65 as the date with some very important and telling arguments in his book: *Redating the New Testament*.

20. The objections which have been brought against it are real, but they are far from being insurmountable; and in any case, other proposed identifications run up against some even greater difficulties (*see* R. E. Brown, *The Gospel According to John*, I (New York: 1966), p. xcviii).

21. The First Epistle of St. John opens with a solemn prologue in which the author, speaking in his own name and in that of his companions, assumes the quality of eyewitness: "Something which has existed since the beginning, that we have heard, and we have seen with our own eyes; that we have watched and touched with our hands: the Word, who is life"? (1:1). This also very forcefully affirms the divinity of Jesus: "We are in the true God, as we are in his Son Jesus Christ. This is the true God, this is Eternal Life" (5:20). But he does not explicitly say that this conviction comes from a teaching of Christ.

22. St. Irenaeus, *Advers, Haeres.*, III, 1:1. The original Greek text is preserved by Eusebius, *Eccl. History*, V, 8:4.

23. In Eusebius, *Eccl. History*, V. 20:5-8.
24. Mention is often made of the gullibleness of St. Irenaeus. Thus in *Adv. Haer.*, II, 22:5, he attributes to the "ancients," who receive it from St. John, the opinion according to which Jesus would have lived for fifty years, having begun his preaching ministry around the age of thirty, according to Luke 3:23. In fact, Irenaeus bases himself especially on John 8:57 ("you haven't even attained fifty years and you have seen Abraham") interpreted too narrowly. And he doesn't say how he gathered the testimony of the ancients. In fact he probably owes this information to Papias, Bishop of Hierapolis, whose information is often suspect. This case is very different from the one with which we are dealing, in which Irenaeus insists as much upon his source, Polycarp, as upon the fidelity of his own recollections. The same should be said about *Adv. Haer.*, V, 5:1; V, 36:1; V, 33:4-5, in which it is a matter of various problems relating to the other world: the various abodes of the elect, and the extraordinary fruitfulness of the new creation. In V, 33:5 the source of Irenaeus is explicitly mentioned: it is actually Papias. And it is more than probable that such is the case for the other text quoted in this note. This is what commentators on St. Irenaeus generally believe. If, on certain points, Irenaeus took his own account of information which he was not able to control, this does not make his own testimony a weak one, when he tells us that he had himself heard St. Polycarp speak of his personal relations with his master, St. John, who recounted to him what he had heard from the very mouth of Jesus.

Chapter VIII

1. See above, pp. 35-36, and see also note 1, 2nd Part, chap. 5.

Chapter IX

1. Even if 16:13 primitively belonged to another source or to another redactional level than the texts in which Jesus teaches his preexistence and his divinity, the contradiction would exist on the level of the final redaction which is very strongly unified, as all commentators recognize.

Chapter X

1. H. Bourgeois, "Nouveaux venus en Christianisme," Ètudes 357 (Dec. 1982), 667-79.
2. H. Bourgeois, art. cit., 675.
3. Above, p. 81.

4. Maurice Blondel, *The Letter on Apologetics and History and Dogma*, (trans. Alexander Dru and Illtyd Trethowan [New York: Holt, Reinhardt and Winston, 1964], pp. 245-46.)

5. Chap. III, par. 13. The text between quotes is a quotation from St. John Chrysostom, Homily 17 on Genesis, PG 53, col. 134. The conciliar text takes its inspiration from the Encyclical of Pius xii, *Divino afflante Spiritu*, 1943.

6. Studies on this point are quite rare and fragmentary. *See* above all H. Pinard, "Les infiltrations paiennes dans l'ancienne loi d'après les Peres de l'Eglise: la thèse de la condescendance," *Rech. Sc. Relig.* 9 (1919), 197-221. *See also* A. Clamer, *Les Nombres, dans la Sainte Bible commentee*, under the direction of L. Pirot and A. Clamer, (Paris: 1940), pp. 231-34. This doctrine is likewise found in Jewish tradition. *See* F. Dreyfus, "La condescendance divine (synkatabasis) comme principe hermeneutique de l'Ancien Testament dans la tradition juive et dans la tradition chretienne," *Actes du Congres de l'Association internationale pour l'Etude de l'Ancien Testament* (Salamanca: 1983).

7. Cf. for example St. John Chrysostom, *Adversus Judaeos*, 4:6, PG 48, col. 880. The fathers especially apply this principle to the permission for divorce (following the word or statement of Jesus in Mt 19:8) and to the law on sacrifices. On this latter point, we find some almost identical considerations in St. John Chrysostom and in the great Jewish theologian, Maimonides, who died in 1204 (*Guide of the Perplexed*, III, 32).

8. *See in particular* "Le probleme de Jesus, considerations sur la distinction de la mentalite et de l'esprit," in *Oeuvres completes, II, Critique religieuse* (Paris: 1968), 576-82. *See also* "Portrait de M. Pouget,"*Oeuvres completes, I, Portraits* (Paris: 1966), p. 163, in which in using a slightly different vocabulary the same idea is expressed: "We call envelopment the state of a germ in which the element of life is found mixed with foreign and opposite elements. From this negative point of view, the development will be the effort made by this germ to free itself. We call spirit the idea which informs and directs the process of development." He had previously correctly remarked: "It is only after the fact that we can thus discern an idea and its envelopment. In reality, the two elements intermingle" (ibid., p. 162).

9. Did Jesus share the mentality of his contemporaries? In principle, being in every way similar to us with the exception of sin, it is necessary to respond affirmatively, entirely, at least, for the positive aspects of this mentality, which are not connected to sin. But here a distinction is called for. Jesus had been *fully* man, but not *middle man*, (in the English sense of middle). Who can deny that Jesus had been an exceptional personality? But the nature of these personalities is precisely to lift themselves above the mentality of their time. Jesus was a man of his time, but he was not a captive of the mentality of his time, which he had strongly contested. On the manner in which

Jesus shared our human condition, *see*, in this work, chap. 11 of the Third Part.

Chapter XI

1. On precomprehension, confer what has been said above, Introduction, no. 2, chap. 1, par. 2, p. 2, and the note 3, ibid.
2. This is what E. Käsemann affirms in *Jesu letzter Wille nach Johannes 17*, 3rd ed. (Tübingen: 1971).
3. Preface to H. Urs von Balthasar, *La Foi du Christ* (Paris: 1968), p. 8.
4. Op. cit. (note 2), p. 181.
5. Origen, *Contra Celsus*, II, 23-24.
6. In the celebrated Letter to Flavius (449), so widely hailed by the Council of Chalcedon (DS 295).

Chapter XII

1. We can read an entire chapter devoted to this subject in J. Pohier, *Quand je dis Dieu* (Paris: 1977), pp. 173-98.
2. St. Thomas Aquinas, *Summa Theologica*, IIIª, quest. 46, art. 6.
3. See the parallel text of Matthew 27:34.
4. This baptism refers to his Passion and death. The parallel text in Mark 10:38 shows this clearly. Exegetes are unanimous on this point. They are less so in affirming that it is a matter of an authentic word of Jesus, but the reasons for which they contest it are not convincing.
5. The translation of the verb *sunechein* is difficult here as in 2 Corinthians 5:14: "The love of Christ urges us on." It concerns a tension, a suffering, an urgent demand which, in some way, prods one on.
6. The great majority of critics think that it is a question there of words actually uttered by Jesus, even if these slight differences between the evangelists do not permit a word-for-word reconstruction.

Chapter XIII

1. In his Commentary on the *Sentences* of Peter Lombard, IIIrd Book, distinction 1, quest. 2, art. 5.
2. One would be gravely mistaken to see in these questions some Byzantine discussions of a decadent scholasticism. The personality of St. Thomas, his genius, his holiness are by themselves alone the guarantee that they are nothing of the kind. If he examines these unreal hypotheses, it is in order to have a better understanding of the various aspects of the *reality*, which Revelation shows us.

3. G. C. Anawati and L. Gardet, *Mystique musulmane, aspects et tendances, experiences et techniques* (Paris: 1961).

4. Cf. op. cit., note 3, p. 33, 110-15; *see also* L. Massignon, *Essai sur les origines et les techniques de la mystique musulmane* (Paris: 1922), especially the texts of Bistami quoted on pp. 249-50.

5. Cf. op. cit., note 3, p. 39; L. Massignon, *Al-Hallaj, martyr mystique de l'Islam* (Paris: 1922), vol. I, pp. 61ff.

6. Cf. op. cit., note 3, p. 60ff., 115-21.

7. The bibliography regarding Eckhart is vast. Confer a good summary of his doctrine by J. Gandillac, "Eckhart et ses disciples," in *Histoire de l'Eglise* under the direction of A. Fliche and V. Martin, t. 13 (Paris: 1951), pp. 377-86.

8. See proposition 13, condemned by the Constitution *In agro dominico* (1329), DS 963.

9. Text quoted by L. Gardet, *La Mystique* (Paris: 1970), p. 71.

10. *De l'union a Dieu*, chap. 12, trans. by J.-J. Berthier, O.P. (Paris: 1896); quoted by L. Gardet, op. cit., p. 67.

11. Confer J. Galot, *La Conscience de Jesus* (Paris-Gembloux: 1971), in the section titled: "La conscience humaine du moi divin" (pp. 132-82), the paragraph: the explanation by mystical experience (pp. 152-67) and the authors whom he quotes.

12. R. Garrigou-Lagrange, *Le Sauveur et son amour pour nous* (Paris: 1934), p. 102.

13. H. Bergson, *Les Deux Sources de la morale et de la religion*, (Paris: 1932), p. 248.

14. Confer the profession of faith exacted from the Copts at the Ecumenical Council of Florence (1442), DS 1330.

15. Within the inner life of the Most Blessed Trinity, the Son is unable to look upon himself if we can employ this rather gross anthropomorphism—for everything which is not a relation between the divine persons is common to the three persons, according to the standard doctrine set forth at the Council of Florence (cf. the preceding note). The look of the Son upon himself would therefore be common to the three persons, which is clearly contradictory. As the human intellectual life of Jesus has, as subject, the divine person of the Son we can, it seems, say the same thing of Jesus in his intelligence as Man, totally empowered by the impulse of love which the Son bears toward the Father.

16. In order not to complicate the exposition and to preserve a relative simplicity for it, we have not spoken of the Holy Spirit, who is himself this total reciprocal gift of the Father and of the Son in true love.

17. The preceding pages owe much to the beautiful book of Louis Bouyer, *The Eternal Son* (New York: 1979), he himself quotes, in the same sense the Protestant theologian Wolfhart Pannenberg, *Grundzüge der Christologie* (Guterslöh: Mohn, 1959) (especially chap. 9).

Chapter XIV

1. St. Augustine, *De diversis quaestionibus*, 60:65, PL 40, col. 60.Regarding the hesitations on this point, confer the authors cited above in note 6 of chap. 2 of the First Part.

2. Declaration of the Holy Office of June 5, 1918, DS 3645.

3. DS 3812.

4. As we have seen, this response is not absolutely unanimous. *See* above, chap. 3, First Part, p. 24.

5. There are the same verbs in Greek for John and for Sirach: *see* (*oran* in both); reveal (*exegoumai*, from which comes exegesis, in St. John; the same verb with the prefix *dia*, in Sirach).

6. If there are prophetic visions which appear to be face-to-face visions of God (Is 6:5; Ez 1; 1 Kings 22), their exceptional and fleeting character is very different from this ordinary and customary knowledge which Jesus claims. Perhaps we would be able to explain, if need be, the affirmations of the Fourth Gospel by admitting, in Jesus of Nazareth, a superior prophetic charism which would be a permanent revelation of the mysteries of God, but would this explanation take into account the assimilation that Jesus constantly is making between his knowledge of God which is eternal and that eternal, divine knowledge of the Father by the Son?

7. *See* P. Vallotton, *Le Christ et la Foi* (Neuchatel-Paris: 1960), which vigorously maintains this interpretation, and previous authors cited by him, who have preceded him in this approach.

8. The question is often raised: In this hypothesis, at what moment did Jesus begin to have the beatific vision? The traditional response, repeated by Pius xii in his encyclical on the *Mystical Body*, is: from the first instant of his existence (cf. DS 3812). But, in any case, it could only be really the object of a human knowledge at the moment in which Jesus would have had the possibility of performing real human acts.

9. Cf. *Summa Theologica* of St. Thomas Aquinas, Iª, quest. 12, art. 2.

10. I have relied rather freely on Jacques Maritain, *L'Intuition créatrice dans l'art et la poèsie* (Paris: 1966). Jacques Maritain himself employed the notions elaborated in this work when, in another book, he studies the beatific vision of Jesus; *see* Jacques Maritain, *De la grace et de l'humanite de Jesus* (Paris: 1967), pp. 50-52, and note 1, p. 51.

11. The classical Catholic doctrine attributes to Christ an "infused knowledge," which is precisely this conceptual knowledge by which Jesus transmits to men "that which he had seen with the Father" (cf. Jn 8:38 and 1:18).

12. M.-J. Nicolas, *Theologie de la Resurrection* (Paris: 1982), p. 75. The text of St. Thomas to which he makes allusion at the end of the quote is the *Summa Theologica*, IIIª, quest. 10, art. 2, corpus. It is true that

after having said that each knows in God everything which concerns him, St. Thomas adds that, given the place and the mission of Christ, everything concerns him, therefore he knows everything. But, Fr. Nicholas rightfully remarks that this reasoning is true only for the Risen Christ, but not for Christ during his earthly existence. I thank Fr. Ponsot, O.P., who pointed out this text of Fr. Nicholas to me.

13. John Maldonatus (1534-83), a Spanish Jesuit, was undoubtedly the greatest exegete of the sixteenth century. The text quoted is found in his commentary on Matthew 26:39.

14. J. Lebreton, *La Vie et L'Enseignement de Jesus-Christ, Notre Seigneur*, II (Paris: 1931), p. 339. English translation: *The Life and Teaching of Jesus Christ, our Lord* (Burns and Oates, 1949), II.

15. The fathers of the Church have insisted on the two human wills of Christ, the natural will, spontaneous inclination of the human will toward happiness, life, joy (in Greek *thelesis*), and free will which deliberates and which chooses (in Greek *boulesis*); see St. Maximus the Confessor (580-622), *Letter to Marin*, PG 91, col. 12 and 13; Application to Christ, ibid., col. 28-29. He is followed by St. John Damascene (675-749), *De fide orthodoxa*, book II, chap. 22, PG 94, col. 944ff., and by the theologians of the Middle Ages, especially St. Thomas who will distinguish the will as nature and the will as reason (*voluntas ut natura, voluntas ut ratio*); cf *Summa theologica*, IIIª, quest. 18, art. 3.

16. *Summa theologica*, IIIª, quest. 18, art. 5.

17. Confer R. d'Ouince, "Le Père Jules Lebreton, 1873-1956," *Les Etudes*, vol. 290 (Sept. 1956), 274-80, especially p. 279ff. For his explanation of the Agony in the Garden, *see* J. Lebreton, *La Vie et L'Enseignement de Notre Seigneur Jesus-Christ*, t. II (Paris: 1931), pp. 311-46. (English translation, *see* above, note 14).

Abbreviations of Sources

These have been reduced to a minimum so as not to bewilder the reader who is not a specialist.

PG 34, col. 3: Greek Patrology (Migne), vol. 34, col. 3.

PL 34, col. 3: Latin Patrology, *idem.*

DS: H. DENZINGER-A. SCHONMETZER, *Enchiridion Symbolorum et declarationum,* 32nd edition, Fribourg-en-Brisgau: 1963.

Strack-Billerbeck: H. L. STRACK and P. BILLERBECK, *Kommentar zum Neuen Testament aus Talmud und Midrasch,* 2nd edition, Munich: 1926 (the standard collection of rabbinic texts with parallels in the New Testament).

T.O.B.: Ecumenical Translation of the Bible, Paris: 1972 (N.T.) and 1975 (O.T.).

B.J.: Jerusalem Bible in one Volume, 2nd edition, Paris: 1973.

References to St. Thomas Aquinas: IIIa, q. 10, a. 4, Corp. = *Summa Theologica,* Third Part, question 10, article 4, in the body of the article.

Short Lexicon

Arians, Arianism: confer p. 15.

agnoetes: see pp. 19ff.

apocalyptic: having to do with revelation (apocalypse) of the cataclysms which will mark the end of the world.

Apocrypha: writings contemporaneous with the books of the Bible, related to them, but which have not been admitted to the list of Inspired Books.

eschatological: having to do with the end of the world (eschatology).

Fundamentalism: interpretation of the Bible which takes everything literally, for example, it will affirm that God created light before the sun (cf. Gn 1:3 and Gn 1:16).

hermeneutic: the science and methodology of interpretation, especially of the Bible.

Johannine: relating to the biblical writings attributed to the apostle St. John by the Church's tradition (Gospels, Epistles, Apocalypse).

Midrash: one of a group of Jewish commentaries on the Hebrew Scriptures written between A.D. 400 and 1200.

Nestorians, Nestorianism: see p. 15.

ontology: division of philosophy having to do with what is common to everything which exists: being.

pericope: short biblical passage forming a unit from the viewpoint of form and content: the pericope of the Wedding at Cana (Jn 2:1-11).

precomprehension: confer p. 87ff.

hypostatic union: union in Jesus of divinity and humanity in the unity of a single Person.

Biblical Citations

—————— OLD TESTAMENT ——————

—————— NEW TESTAMENT ——————

149

Authors Cited

COUNCILS